DIRT ROADS AND DAYDREAMS

Peggy,
"Happy Trails to you!"
Dave Brown
2012

DAVE BROWN

Wasteland Press
www.wastelandpresss.net
Shelbyville, KY USA

Dirt Roads and Daydreams
by Dave Brown

Copyright © 2011 Dave Brown
ALL RIGHTS RESERVED

First Printing – July 2011
ISBN: 978-1-60047-591-7
Library of Congress Control Number: 2011931699

NO PART OF THIS BOOK MAY BE REPRODUCED IN ANY FORM, BY PHOTOCOPYING OR BY ANY ELECTRONIC OR MECHANICAL MEANS, INCLUDING INFORMATION STORAGE OR RETRIEVAL SYSTEMS, WITHOUT PERMISSION IN WRITING FROM THE COPYRIGHT OWNER/AUTHOR

Printed in the U.S.A.

0 1 2 3 4 5 6 7 8 9

To my wife, Sheri (aka "Beans") ... I love you more than baseball.

CONTENTS

FOREWORD	ix
Introduction	1
Dirt Roads and Daydreams	3
Joe Wanted to Grow Up to Be an Alligator	9
"Phil" Didn't Look Like a Ricky	15
Three Sunday Nights in February	24
Sleepless in Atlanta	28
The Box Cutter Made Me Do It	32
A Humble Wagon, A Haunting Song	37
"The Tie that Binds"	43
An Extraordinary, Ordinary Man	49
Daddy … My Hero	53
Do-Be, Do-Be, Do	59
To All the Oysters I've Loved Before	66
One Golf Swing and Other Important Stuff	69
Sterile as a Stainless Steel Operating Table	74
The "Spumoni" of My Life	78
Mickey Mantle, My Boys and Me	83
"Do Yourself a Favor, Take a Kid Fishing"	89
"Cancer? … Did My Doctor Just Say Cancer?"	95
"Don't Let Go … Just Hang On!"	102
"FREE KITTENS!"	107
"Just Feed 'em Cantaloupe!"	111
Traveling Light, Wanderlust and "Muffin"	114
"Somebody Bet on the Gray"	121
A Multi-Colored Yellow Jacket	127
The Third Time was the Charm	132
The Road Back	137

So … You Don't Think You'd Miss a Cat?	141
"Somewhere Over the Rainbow" … is a Cabin at Big Canoe	145
Denominations, Autumn Leaves, and the "Group Dynamic"	149
"Now, THIS is What a Mountain Cabin is Supposed to Look Like!"	153
Restoration	158
"Cosmo" and "Pinky"	167
Back Home Again with Evinrude	171
"Oreo" … not the Nabisco Cookie	175
Old School vs. New School	178
Collard Greens, Sausage, and Septic Tanks	185
Uncle Charlie's Magical Mystery Tour	192
"Thanks for Giving a Damn"	197

DIRT ROADS AND DAYDREAMS

FOREWORD

Have you ever begged a parent or a grandparent to "Tell me a story, please"? If so, this book from my friend Dave Brown will bring joy to your heart, laughter to lighten your troubled day, appreciation of homespun humor, as well as an appreciation of the friends who are life coaches and protectors.

These stories chronicle the day-to-day life of a family with all the participants playing the normal roles in life. David's family and friends are very much like those in yours and mine ... all so different, yet each one playing such major roles in the lives of all they touch. They, with all their idiosyncrasies, are what color the tapestry of life with fun and pleasure as well as sadness and grief. The blend provides a compelling, poignant and delightful sight to behold.

David has an indomitable spirit that inspires others. He is an extraordinary person. He survived mid-life terminal brain cancer, twenty surgeries, divorce, depression ... he has survived to love and marry again and relishes a second chance. His wit, wisdom, cheerful disposition and courage are an inspiration.

Your own family story needs to be told, just as the human drama and the working of God is told in the Old Testament. Do as Dave has done and bless your family with stories about grandparents, parents, aunts and uncles so that the young can see the threads of fears, hopes and dreams and be blessed.

This book is a blessing waiting to be received by all who read it.

~ Dr. Bill Self

Introduction

In one scene in the movie *Grumpier Old Men*, Burgess Meredith rambles on and on for no apparent reason and then just stops mid-sentence and chuckles. After waiting a moment for Meredith to continue Jack Lemmon prompts him by saying, "So Dad, what's your point". Meredith scoffs at him as he gleefully explains, "There ain't any point ... I just like telling stories".

First of all thanks if you actually bought this book (I've been told I'll make a couple of bucks if anyone actually buys one). If I sell five of them, I'm planning to get a haircut. Okay, before you turn another page it's important to get this in your head. Hemingway or Grizzard, I ain't. I'm no writer ... I just like telling stories.

So why did I spend the last two years of my life writing stories about stuff that I've experienced? I'll be damned if I know, maybe it was a calling ... who knows? I've just had all these things bouncing around in what's left of my brain for so long I thought I'd write all of it down.

Fifteen years ago I was diagnosed with a cancerous brain tumor. I have been very fortunate and have survived what is usually a fatal diagnosis. I can't possibly offer any explanation for why I survived when so many others have not. I simply continue to live one day at a time, humbly thankful for the gift of continued life. Surviving cancer, however, does not mean that the suffering ends and everything is back to normal. The long-term effects of the chemotherapy and radiation treatments that saved my life have extracted their toll on me and everything on me except the baby toe on my left foot has either been replaced or rebuilt. I was able to work full time for many years for which I am grateful. When putting in a full day at the office got to be too much, I knew it was time to retire.

I spent my first year of retirement reflecting on my life; and in the process identified five important things that have sustained me through the easy and not-so-easy times. Faith, family, friends, fun, and free enterprise … hmmm, lots of words that started with the letter "F". I call them, "The Five F's". Brilliant, eh? In retrospect, it's where I invested my life. That investment has yielded the invaluable return of priceless memories and the peace of mind and hope that my faith offers. Time, memories, and hope … do we really, truly own anything more precious?

This book contains a collection of true stories and reflections about my "Five F's". Many of the stories have relevance to one another and some are completely autonomous. Heck, you'll even meet and get to know our dog, Oreo and my old tomcat Evinrude. The underlying theme behind all of the stories you'll read is how they've have helped me through adversity, especially my battle with cancer, and defined who I am today. I can only hope that my experiences can help you or perhaps anyone you know or love who has been in a similar situation as mine.

I knew if I wanted to leave something as permanent as a book of reflections on how I dealt with adversity, I would have to expose some of my most personal thoughts, actions, habits, and ultimately, my character. Life has not always been a bowl of cherries. Life has been a series of struggles. I have not always made the best decisions. Sometimes, I was a "Grade A" dumb-ass. You will read about some of my failures. However, regardless of the decisions I have made … I have always felt loved. Through faith, patience and perseverance, my life has rebounded with happiness and contentment beyond my highest dreams.

In summary, I'm a storyteller. Here are a few. I hope at least one of them makes you smile.

Dirt Roads and Daydreams

I grew up in a little house on a dirt road.

Our house was heated in the winter with a coal-burning fireplace and cooled in the summer by the occasional breeze blowing through the opened windows. An old-fashioned wringer washer graced the back porch and the clean laundry hung drying in the sun on a clothesline in the back yard. Life was simple there. Nintendo, X-Box and PlayStation hadn't been invented yet. My favorite toys were my Mama's pots and pans and whatever stick I most recently picked up from the yard.

I was my parents' first child.

My first memories were made in the little house on the dirt road. My first steps were taken there. My first meal was eaten there. My first word, "Bug," was spoken there. My first smell of a fresh cedar Christmas tree cut from the nearby woods was enjoyed there. My first birthday was celebrated there. My first pet, a duck named "Blue," was raised there.

Blue was actually blue when we got him so I creatively named him "Blue". He was one of those dyed Easter ducks from back in the 1950s that usually live only a week or two because of the dye. Not Blue. I think he lived more than ten years. That darn duck was indestructible. Of course he turned white after a couple of weeks but we still called him Blue. He wouldn't answer to anything else. Blue was our guard duck. He could make more noise than a scared Chihuahua and had a particular aversion to snakes. Out in the country, there are harmless snakes everywhere. My

Mama's greatest fear was that a snake would come into the yard while I was outside playing and bite me and I would instantly drop dead. With Blue in the yard, I was safe. Blue wouldn't allow a snake anywhere near our house. Have you ever seen a duck eat a snake? As soon as a snake would show up in our yard, that dang duck would swallow it whole—the head, the tail, the whole damn thing. He was a snake-eating machine. Mama always felt safe with me outside as long as Blue was around. I always felt safe inside knowing Blue was on guard just on the other side of the screen door.

I learned to daydream staring through the screen door of the front porch. I have never gotten over it. I still enjoy staring through windows and screens at nothing, lost in the world of my own thoughts, daydreaming about imagined adventures yet to come.

Lying on my back in the grass while gazing skyward considering the clouds, I could smell the rich earth, the rain, and experience the sights, sounds, and smells of the countryside (along with the occasional fresh duck poop). From the "caw, caw, caw" of the passing crows, the quacking of Blue running something out of the yard, the evening symphonies of the crickets and frogs, to the whistle of a distant train, my future passions were fueled by the sights and sounds of the countryside.

Three or four times a year the county sent a road crew with a larger-than-life machine to scrape the rural dirt road. With each pass it unearthed jewels and left them scattered along the sides of the road. I couldn't wait for the road scraper. Quartz, granite, and shale were all diamonds, rubies, and emeralds to me.

After a summer rain, there were mud pies and countless puddles to enjoy. I panned for gold in those puddles. Using my Mama's tin pie pans, I separated the gravel from the gold. My gold was a quartz crystal. I discovered several through the years. I still have them and they are still jewels to me.

It was in that little house on the dirt road that I fell in love with my family.

Mama and Daddy met after the war while Dad was in Atlanta visiting friends from Connecticut. Dad returned home and began corresponding with Mama through the mail. Real handwritten letters you could hold and re-read over and over again. Don't you love to get a handwritten letter in the mail? They fell in love through those letters. After what my Mom's father labeled a "mail order romance," they were married in 1950 and became Lee and Helen Brown.

Daddy was like Mark Twain's proverbial Connecticut Yankee, a devoted subject in my mother's Georgian court. After having bravely charged up the sands of Omaha Beach in Normandy, a decorated D-Day Ranger, my Dad was swept off his feet by a petite Southern Belle. Two years later, on a crisp October morning, I arrived … David Tribble Brown.

They were so happy then. Over sixty years later, they still are.

Each day Mom and Dad drove to work together on a long and lonely road to Atlanta. They left in the dark and they returned in the dark. We lived just down the dirt road from my grandparents so I stayed with them during the week. My parents were tireless in their efforts to improve our options in life. Their actions taught me about setting goals and the reward of a dedicated work ethic.

During the week at Granny's house, I woke every morning to her singing.

She had the sweetest soprano voice and was always singing hymns or popular songs of the day. Granny taught me that singing was a source of happiness. Singing all the while, she taught me patience as I watched her meticulously work her vegetable gardens from the spring planting until the fall harvest. If she saw a snake in the yard, she would go after it with a hoe. Granny hated snakes just as much as Blue.

PaPa had a little country store at the end of the dirt road. When I say "little," I do mean little. It had one gas pump, a candy counter, a non-electric ice box; it was heated by a pot-bellied stove, cooled by open windows, and the walls were lined with varied and sundry dry goods.

The local folks were his customers. Everyone loved PaPa; his customers were really his friends. Mostly they came to visit. Sure, they picked up what they needed while they were there, but that was not the primary goal. They sat around the pot-bellied stove in the winter and under the covered porch in the front of the building in the summer. The driveway and porch floor were paved with discarded bottle caps. PaPa had a grand sense of humor and rare was day when someone wasn't sitting there listening to his stories. Stories and jokes were plentiful. Being around PaPa in his store taught me how to laugh, how to listen, and most importantly, he taught me how to enjoy telling a tale. Listening to PaPa tell a tale was like watching an artist paint a masterpiece. His homespun humor, impeccable sense of timing, and the colloquial delivery of his stories kept his store full of friends.

Mama had three brothers, Uncle Rudolph, Uncle "H," and Uncle Sam. All of my aunts and uncles lived close to us so we were not only family, we were neighbors as well. Each of Mama's brothers had children before I was born. All girls. My cousins, Mary Ann, Beth, Melody, and Cherry, were born throughout the five-year period before me. I was the first grandson, the first nephew, and the first male cousin in our family and was the beneficiary of added attention as a result of my fortunate gender.

My Uncle Rudolph introduced me to the world away from the dirt roads.

He showed me the stars and planets through his telescope. We gazed together at the "rings" of Saturn, the craters on the moon, the "red eye" on Jupiter, and beyond. Uncle Rudolph introduced me to Heaven as a place beyond the stars, a place to which he would be called all too soon. He was only forty-seven when he died of cancer.

His wife, Aunt Evelyn, was alone with five children, all under the age of sixteen—Beth, Cherry, Louise, Pam, and the youngest, Rudolph, Jr. Rudy doesn't even remember his Daddy, but there was never a prouder father of a son. They have all grown to be fine adults. Aunt Evelyn never remarried. She had to be the mother and the father to their five children from the day she lost him in 1965. Amazing. Uncle Rudolph would be so proud of all of them, especially Aunt Evelyn. He taught me to dream and never hesitate to look to places far beyond the dirt roads.

My Uncle "H" lovingly played with me.

His love was relentless. He was forever tickling me by "counting my ribs" and making me laugh. I always thought of Uncle "H" as a man's man. I thought of him as being tough as nails (even though I knew he was as soft as a feather). Honestly, he scared the hell out of me every time I saw him but I loved him to death and couldn't wait to see him again. He would always look at me and say, "Where's my knife?" Subliminally, I feared the worst. Maybe he was referring to my testicles. After all, at this point in my life, it appeared to me they served no apparent purpose and as far as I knew were expendable. Although I didn't know why, I was sure I wanted to keep them.

When I got a little older, he taught me how to use that legendary pocketknife. At just the right age, he gave me my first pocketknife. It was a blue Cub Scout knife. He showed me how to whittle on a piece of wood. I whittled very important art pieces under his supervision. Well, maybe they weren't really important pieces of art, but he would always see the art in my effort. He taught me how to hold the knife with the blade open and toss it so it would always stick in the target. Eventually, my little brother Phil made a pretty good target. To this day he claims every scar on his body came from my pocketknife. He is prone to exaggeration. Well, maybe just a few of his scars were my fault. I have always carried a pocketknife because of Uncle "H". I have given away dozens of pocketknives to kids wherever we lived, always explaining how the toughest man I knew would have wanted them to have one.

Uncle "H" was ambidextrous. He could draw, write, or throw with either hand. We threw baseballs, footballs, tennis balls, rubber balls, well ... just about anything, 'round to one another outside and even inside the house. We never broke a thing. He never missed and neither did I.

He was married to Aunt Ann (the craziest, most happy and positive person from my childhood). Mary Ann is their daughter, my oldest cousin, and she will always be "Cuz" to me. Uncle "H" spent time with me ... lots of time. He taught me how to giggle ... that's a lot different than laughing. He taught me how to play. He taught me how to give. Uncle "H" was my buddy. He still is.

My Uncle Sam taught me that work was fun.

He let me help him wash and wax his car. Over and over again he patiently showed me the right way to do it. Over and over again he watched me try to do it better and encouraged me as I continued to improve. As a young teenager, he let me do his entire car all by myself. We were both proud that day, even though looking back ... well, it felt a little like Tom Sawyer whitewashing fences. Uncle Sam was pretty dang smart. He and Aunt Eris had three children, Melody, Diane, and my first male cousin, Sammy. He taught me how to take care of things. He taught me how to appreciate the results of hard work.

Together, my uncles taught me a song about a little bird sitting up on a telegraph pole that involved some rather suggestive phrasing. *"Little birdie, little birdie, flew up on a telegraph pole. He ruffled up his neck and he ..."*, well, let's just say they taught me how to get attention. I still sing that song. It still gets attention.

My older girl cousins, Mary Ann, Beth, Melody, and Cherry, considered me their own personal baby doll. I was a veritable cuddly puppy that you constantly spent time petting. They spoiled me rotten, just ruined me. They taught me the value of affection ... how to give and how to receive affection. They will never know how their love shaped who I've become. They helped mold my heart. Did I mention anything about being spoiled rotten?

Our families spent so much time together. We always did. Nearly every Sunday afternoon until I was grown was spent at PaPa and Granny's house with my family. I have walked hand-in-hand daydreaming with each of these wonderful family members on our dirt road. Some are gone, some remain; our dirt roads and daydreams have bound us together forever.

Joe Wanted to Grow Up to Be an Alligator

> "There is no friend like an old friend…"
> ~ Oliver Wendell Holmes

When I was a kid, a half-gallon of ice cream was packaged in a cardboard container like a couple of bricks stacked on top of one another.

In 1956, Mama and Daddy bought their first house in Chamblee, Georgia (a suburb of Atlanta). The three of us moved about forty miles away from the little house on the dirt road in Forsyth County that my PaPa provided for them as they were getting their start in their marriage. I was four years old when we moved. Houses were closer together away from the dirt road. Uncle "H" and Aunt Ann soon moved into the house behind us. Their back yard joined ours so we were neighbors.

It was there that I met my new next-door neighbors, Tommy and Joe McCloskey. Tommy was my age and Joe was almost two years younger. Tommy would become the best friend of my childhood. Uncle "H" always told me that Tommy and Joe were direct descendants of the devil himself. According to him, they were as mean as snakes.

Mean as snakes, huh? I knew how to deal with snakes. Just sic old "Blue" on 'em! My pet duck, Blue the snake-eating duck, didn't move with us to Chamblee to defend me, he remained behind … I had to learn to fend for myself. I learned fast.

Two of them and only one of me led to some pretty hefty conflicts in and around the sandbox and on the tire swing. I learned real fast that with them, blood was indeed thicker than water. You see, back in the 1950s there were no such things as plastic sandbox tools and buckets. Everything was made of metal, and sandbox tools made great weapons. I still have the scars to prove it. On top of the hand tools, Joe was bad to bite. You always had to watch your back with Joe ... he'd sneak right up and just bite the hell out of you.

I have a scar on my leg from when we were playing "Cowboys and Indians." One of them shot me in the leg with a bow and arrow. I was the cowboy. They were the Indians. My *Mattel Fanner 50 six-shooter* was a toy pistol. Their bows and target arrows were real. What is a little blood when you're having fun, huh? I told Mama that I fell on a stick in the woods. She bought it.

We were a rowdy bunch. Slugging it out with them through the years didn't hurt me a bit, though, and thinking about it now makes me understand why and from where a lot of my drive evolved. I didn't want to die at their hands as a child. I became a survivor out of necessity.

I remember a time when Joe nearly lost his family jewels on a heavy punching bag that was suspended from a tree on a rope with a very large hook. It was a 100-pound Everlast bag. The logic was for us to hit it instead of each other. We grew up in the day when Rocky Marciano was the "World Heavyweight Boxing Champion." In 1956, Rocky held the most revered individual title in professional sports, so naturally we all wanted to be like him.

On this particular day, Joe was bored and decided it would be fun to climb the rope and slide back down. He climbed up and proceeded to slide down, catching his privates on the very large hook and ripping ... well, some very important anatomy. The sight of Joe's blood, more than usual, sent the three of us screaming into the house to find Tommy and Joe's mom, Betty. Betty threw all three of us into her station wagon and rushed us down the street to Doctor Freeman's office. Doctor Freeman took one look at Joe, told Betty he was going to need stitches, and pulled out the longest needle we had ever seen and prepared to numb Joe for the procedure. Tommy, seeing the size of that needle, climbed up Doctor Freeman's cabinets like a monkey and perched on top of them, close to the ceiling, and refused to come down. Tommy was convinced he was next and would not come down until Doctor Freeman left the room. I guess Doctor Freeman did a good job, because Joe is now the father of his own wild bunch. Doctor Freeman laughed until the day he died about Tommy scaling that wall and perching on the top of the cabinet like a parakeet.

Betty, who someday should be sainted, was Tommy and Joe's mama. Betty was the only mom in the neighborhood with her own car, a four-door 1955 dark green Chevrolet station wagon. A station wagon back then was like a pickup truck with a camper top. There wasn't a seat behind the second row, just a cavernous opening with a roof over it. We would all ride in the very back of the car where we could make faces at the people behind us and stick our heads and feet out the back window. Seat belts hadn't been invented yet, so we were free to move around.

Betty McCloskey was a wonderful person. I think Betty just loved watching us cut up. She would laugh the loudest at our antics. She took it upon herself to give some of the other mothers in the neighborhood a break from their rowdy children. Betty would load up all of the kids several times a year in the back of the station wagon for a "field trip." It didn't matter how many of us there were, she would take us all. We were crammed in there like cord wood and couldn't have been happier. It was just what people did back then. Safety was not something any of us ever thought about.

God bless Betty ... she would regularly take Tommy, Joe, and me to the WSB-TV studio in Atlanta, where they had a live television production every weekday afternoon at 5:00 called *Officer Don and the Popeye Club*. The host was a local beloved personality, "Officer Don." It was a compilation of old spinach-eating "Popeye the Sailor" cartoons, goofy games (like the legendary "Ooey Gooey" bag, where Officer Don was always the brunt of the joke), and recognition of any kid with a birthday. All of the kids attending sat in a section on the set in front of the camera for the entire thirty-minute broadcast.

When the time came during the show for birthday recognitions, Tommy, Joe, and I would always raise our hands proclaiming it was our birthday. It didn't matter what day it was, it was always our birthday. Verification of your actual birthday was never considered necessary and Betty just laughed at the three of us trying to get away with something that surely must have been so obvious. Each of us would march right up and tell Officer Don what we wanted to be when we grew up. (That privilege was reserved for the kids who were having a birthday and it was the only question he ever asked). Tommy and I responded to Officer Don with typical answers you would expect to hear from little boys growing up in the fifties ... things like, Policeman, Fireman, Baseball Player, General, Colonel, Sergeant, stuff like that.

Joe was the last in line that day and when Officer Don asked him what he wanted to be when he grew up, Joe responded, "I want to be an alligator." He meant it.

Officer Don laughed so hard he totally lost control of himself and had to get up and walk away. Everyone on the set was laughing and Joe was laughing as hard as anybody there and didn't even know why. But he really meant it ... he wanted to grow up to be an alligator. He certainly had the teeth for it. He always loved to bite. Uncle "H" always said the McCloskey boys were mean.

When it was your birthday, Officer Don would give you a half-gallon of Atlanta Dairies ice cream to take home with you. When we left the studio, the ice cream was always frozen as solid as a rock. Most of the time our ice cream made it home just fine but I remember returning home one hot summer afternoon when we encountered a rare traffic jam and all three of the cartons of ice cream melted in the back of Betty's station wagon. There was no air conditioning in a 1955 Chevy station wagon.

After getting home and getting the car cleaned up, Tommy and I thought up a joke we could play on Joe. Joe always slept late; Tommy and I didn't. The next day, Tommy and I took one of the empty cardboard ice cream containers, cleaned it up, and filled it with two bricks. Back when we were growing up, everyone had a pile of bricks just laying around in the yard. I never wondered why the bricks were there; they just were. The two bricks fit into the ice cream box like a glove. We hid the carton in Betty's freezer so it would be nice and cold when we presented it to Joe. We would wait until just the right time to give it to him, a time when ice cream would sound like the best thing in the world.

Our trap was set.

After playing outside in the hot sun all day, we gave the "brick" ice cream to Joe at about 3:00 that afternoon, assuring him that it was just for him. When he finally realized that he was not going to indulge in a treat, he got so mad at us that he chased us into the woods and throughout the neighborhood until dark.

By this time in our lives, Joe was bigger than Tommy and me. Heck, Joe was bigger than most men by then. But thankfully he was slower, too.

Somewhere in those woods today are both of those bricks. Joe chased us through those woods carrying the bricks screaming at the top of his lungs exactly where he intended to hit us. When he realized he couldn't catch us, he just threw those bricks at us.

Tommy and I survived.

We lived next door to Tommy and Joe for a total of nine years. They were my closest friends. Tommy was my best friend.

We moved to another house a mile away in 1965 to accommodate the growth of our family. My baby brother Phil, who had arrived in 1957, needed a bedroom of his own. 1965 was the last year of my daily adventures with Tommy and Joe. They were so much fun. Even though Tommy, Joe and I went on to high school together and Tommy and I graduated in the same class at Chamblee High School, my childhood was never the same. It was as though a part of me died. Moving a kid, even once, affects them. Even though it was only a mile away, a mile is a lot farther than fifty feet to go see your best friend when you are a kid.

I dreamed about Tommy and Joe last night.

Tommy's birthday would have been tomorrow. He would have been fifty-eight. Over twenty years ago, Tommy was in a terrible accident and was killed.

Oh, how I wish I could carry my old friend a half-gallon of ice cream and share a piece of birthday cake together.

"Phil" Didn't Look Like a Ricky

> "What's in a name?"
> ~ William Shakespeare

I wanted to name him Ricky.

The Cleavers of the 1950s *Leave It to Beaver* television show seemed to have it all figured out. Dad and Mom would be "Ward and June" and I would be "Wally." However, my baby brother would not be "The Beaver."

He would be "Ricky."

Mama, Daddy, and I lived in a little house with two bedrooms. If the Cleavers had more than two bedrooms, I never saw them on the show. We were set for Ricky's arrival. Ricky and I would sleep in the same bedroom. I slept by myself in a full-size bed. We could sleep together, I thought. And maybe we could even get twin beds like Wally and The Beaver when Ricky got big enough. We would only bathe when were forced to do so and we would never brush our teeth.

Life would be perfect.

Once Ricky learned how to go to the bathroom alone, walk, talk, eat without help, dress and tie his own shoes by himself, I would teach him about the most important thing in the world.

Baseball.

I would show him how to play. I would introduce him to all the great Major League players. I would explain how to calculate their batting averages and what RBIs and ERAs are. I would show him how every player took his stance in the batter's box. Our favorite team would be the Yankees. Ricky's favorite player would be the same as mine, Mickey Mantle. I would tell him just how strong and fast Mickey was.

I would read to him from the little orange hardcover book Dad kept on his nightstand . . . sportswriter Paul Gallico's 1942 classic, *Lou Gehrig: The Pride of the Yankees*. I would explain that Gehrig was Dad's favorite player when he was a boy. I would tell him, as Dad told me, how strong and brave Gehrig was. How Babe Ruth couldn't have been Babe Ruth and compiled all of his records without Lou Gehrig hitting behind him and protecting him in the Yankee lineup. How Gehrig died at thirty-seven, when Dad was only sixteen.

I would teach him all about the history of the game and all of the legends that have gone before.

I would tell him about Dad being in the war and being involved in a battle called D-Day on a place called Omaha Beach in Normandy, France. I would explain that Dad was only nineteen years old when he went to war.

I would tell him about how Mama sings all the time, loves to cook, loves to have folks over to eat meals, and loves to rock babies. I would explain to him that Mom and Dad met at a spaghetti supper in Atlanta when Dad was visiting from his home in Connecticut.

I would excitedly inform him that our PaPa Tribble, Mama's daddy, has a little country store with a pot-bellied stove and that when we went to see him we always got a candy bar. Ricky would love candy bars.

When the neighborhood gang got together for a baseball game, I would always pick Ricky for my team and we would always win.

I would show him how to make a sand castle in our sand box, how to find four leaf clovers for good luck, how to pick wild blackberries and not get chiggers, how to dig in the dirt and find all sorts of jewels to give to Mama.

We would talk and dream of vacations in faraway lands like Florida.

We would lie in the grass and watch the clouds during the day and the stars at night, wait for the rain and its refreshing smell, wonder about God, angels, and stuff like that.

We would have picnics in our yard and maybe we could get our own swing set. We would help Daddy dig out the area in the basement so he could hang his yard tools there.

We would get a dog; maybe Mama would surprise us with it one day after school ... a friendly little bob-tailed female mutt named "Freckles."

All of us would love Freckles forever.

When our folks balked at letting us have a cat, we'd concoct a scheme to tell Mom that we'd gotten a cat before she got home from work. She'd handle Dad. Then we would drive around together until we found one just like we wanted and get home just before Mom and Dad.

We'd name the kitten "Topaz" and declare it to be a magical cat.

We'd explore the neighborhood together. We'd wade in the creeks. We'd walk to school together. We'd go to church together. We'd learn to swim together. We'd go to camp together.

I would dare anybody to mess with Ricky ... the thought of it raises the hair on the back of my neck. I would always have his back. I would always defend him, right or wrong. He's my brother; that's what big brothers do, right?

We'd be in each other's weddings. We'd be favorite uncles to each other's kids.

I couldn't wait for Ricky to arrive.

The summer before his birth in August I went and stayed with PaPa and Granny Tribble at their house to ease the rigors of everyday life for Mom as her pregnancy approached full term.

The call came on a bright August morning. The baby boy had arrived. My Granny handed me the phone and said it was Mama and Daddy. When I got on the phone, they explained that my baby brother had arrived and that they would be home with him soon. I only had one question.

What did you name him?

"Phil," came their reply.

Silence.

I burst into tears and pled my case for a name change. Having learned that it was too late, I said goodbye and waited for their arrival with ... Phil.

They arrived later in the day and I took my first peek at him. They asked me if I would like to hold him, and in our first moments together gazing into each other's eyes I had a revelation. Phil didn't look like a Ricky ... he looked like a Phil.

Phil and I slept in that full-size bed together in our little two-bedroom house until I went to high school. Our little bedroom didn't have room for twin beds.

When I went to high school, Mama and Daddy thought we should each have our own rooms. We moved to another house just down the road with three bedrooms, so Phil and I could each have our own bedroom.

One of the two bedrooms had new twin beds.

This was to be Phil's room.

I never moved into my new room.

I slept in Phil's extra twin bed until I left home for college five years later.

"Goodnight Irene, Goodnight Irene...
I'll See You in My Dreams"

"I love every one of my cousins. They are like brothers and sisters to me."
 ~ Helen Tribble Brown

We loved each other for fifty-five years. Our relationship began when I was three. She was forty at the time. It was 1955.

We laughed along with one another for over half a century.

She loved to tell me the exact day I stole her heart. I've heard the story hundreds of times; I never tire of hearing her tell it.

As a child, I stayed with Mama's folks, PaPa and Granny, during the week until I entered school. Mama and Daddy left before dawn for the drive to Atlanta each day for work and didn't return until after dark.

Every morning, PaPa walked down the dirt road in front of their house to his little country store. After I got up, Granny made me breakfast and I'd watch TV until the daily Tarzan movie on *Armchair Playhouse* was over. Shortly following the movie, Granny and I would walk down to see PaPa at the store, carrying him a freshly made "cathead" biscuit with something homemade inside of it. We'd always be there by ten o'clock. It was our daily routine.

One morning after a particularly intense Tarzan movie involving Johnny Weissmuller saving the entire African continent from a large pride of rogue lions, my three-year-old imagination ran a little wild. Granny came into the living room where I was watching TV and found me perched like a parrot on the back of the sofa, gazing out of the big window with concern about the possibilities of an approaching menace. Granny approached me as I remained on lookout for any potential danger and asked, "What you-a-doin' up on the back of that couch?" ... I innocently responded (at three), "I'm trying to get away from those damned lions!"

Granny tried her best not to burst into laughter ... she failed.

She was laughing so hard she cried and had to sit down in a chair next to the phone. As she sat down the phone began to ring. When she said "hello" everything became funnier to her and the caller on the other end of the line became tickled at her uncontrollable laughter so much that she joined in with Granny.

The laughing caller was Irene.

Irene was Granny and PaPa's niece and Uncle Charlie's youngest daughter. Her mother had died when Irene was very young. She called Granny often.

She was simply calling to check on Granny and see how I was doing. When Granny explained to Irene the reason she was laughing, their laughter began all over again.

Mama had three brothers, who had a combined total of four baby girls between their families before I, the lone male child, came along. My uncles had frills and curls galore. They always wanted a little boy to teach the spicier side of life. By the time I was three, I knew every word that George Carlin would declare decades later unfit for TV. Granny and Irene knew all about their intentions. Today was the first evidence that my uncles had been successful in their efforts to subtly expose me to the ways of the world.

Granny and Irene laughed about it until Granny died in 1980.

Irene and I laughed about it for the rest of her life.

She lived ninety-five years and I've never known a happier soul.

I loved her every day of my life since I realized who she was ... Irene Belle Tribble Bagby.

She didn't like her middle name, Belle. She said it always made her feel like a ding-a-ling.

Irene loved nothing more than laughing, but she was feisty. She didn't use profanity, yet her favorite word was "shit." "Shit," she insisted, was just a slang word, and there was absolutely nothing profane about it. No different than "heck." She explained to every pastor that she ever had that this was the case and would not hear of it being any other way. Rather than risk her feisty side, her preachers just seemed to get tickled with her as she explained her rules. See, Irene had a direct line to Jesus … and all of her church members let the pastors know in advance of Irene and her wit and wisdom.

Irene married Wally Bagby when she was about thirty years old. Wally was twelve years older than her and they adored each other. He died in 1976, thirty-two years after their marriage. Irene outlived him by thirty-four years and never stopped talking about how much she loved Wally.

Although they were never able to have children, I knew Wally as an older guy who loved to make a kid laugh. Irene knew Wally as an older guy who loved her and loved to make her laugh. They were made for each other. There was rarely a dull moment and laughter was the harmony of their life together.

Wally was a prankster his whole life.

His brother told me that back on a Sunday evening in 1938, before Wally and Irene were married, millions of people across the country were shocked when a radio alert from Orson Welles announced that Martians were invading the northeastern part of the nation. Pandemonium reigned for a short period of time before the truth could be told. As is now well known, it was only Welles doing a play adaptation of H. G. Wells' book, *War of the Worlds*.

The national escapade was all Wally needed.

Wally had a "bob-tailed" pet monkey named "Ed." Wally remained single until he was in his forties. His monkey would go along with anything Wally had in mind as long as bananas, grapes, or apples were involved. He and his monkey had been roommates for years. What Wally had in mind this time was some serious mischief ... he bought a quart of bright green paint and painted Ed with two good coats of it 'til old Ed was a bright green color. The week after the hullabaloo over the false Martian invasion, Wally took his new "Martian Monkey" into town right before dusk. He turned Ed loose in downtown Buford. Wally then called the local radio station and reported the sighting of a Martian in town. There were over a dozen witnesses that confirmed the sighting. It made the regional news. Wally listened to it all on the radio as Ed was getting a good scrubbing along with his well-earned bowl of fruit. As far as I know, only close family members knew it was Wally and his monkey.

After Wally died in 1976, Irene decided it was time for her to learn how to drive. She was in her sixties.

She bought a little Ford Maverick and could be seen zipping to and fro from their home in Buford throughout Forsyth County, where so many of her Tribble family members lived. She was forever visiting her aunts, uncles, and cousins. Everyone loved Irene and all of her family were tickled that she had decided to learn to drive so they could see her more often.

One day while she was circling the Forsyth County courthouse in her car, the little Maverick stalled right in the middle of an intersection. Her cousin Weldon saw that she was having trouble and began to walk from several blocks away to her aid. As he walked, he watched her repeatedly try to crank the car without success. All the while, an old man wearing overalls in a pickup truck on her bumper continually blew his horn at her trying to urge her out of his way.

Before Weldon could make it to assist her, Irene had had enough of the old man and his horn. She took her keys out of the ignition and marched back to the pickup truck behind her with its horn still blaring and confronted her nemesis, informing him (in no uncertain terms) that she would gladly let him to go and try to get her car cranked while she sat behind him and blew "the damn horn" for him! I'm thinking that "damn" is probably another one of those slang words she told the preachers about, too.

From a close position just outside Irene's line of sight, her cousin Weldon laughed until he cried. Her confrontation with "Horatio the horn blower," as she called her courthouse nemesis, was to become legendary amongst her Tribble family cousins. Weldon told the story all over the county for years and tears of laughter never failed to flow.

About five years ago, Irene realized that it was time to take residence in a nursing home care facility. Just like any other obstacle I'd ever seen her face, she took it head-on and decided to be happy.

And happy she was.

I called her on the phone several times every week for brief, sassy visits reminiscing about "damned lions," "Martian monkeys," and blowing "the damn horn" at stalled cars. I went to see her often (though never enough). Each time both of us declared what a wonderful life we've both had, thankful for our survival, how we've been lucky to laugh so much and still remember simple things … like our names.

A couple weeks ago her niece Berma stopped as she approached Irene's door.

She could hear her praying.

As she prayed, Berma listened as Irene asked God to let her time be near as she was longing so to see her mother. She expressed with a grateful heart her thankfulness for her life, love, and laughter.

Her laughter finally stopped last Thursday night. She was ninety-five years old.

And everyone who knew Irene cried . . . until they laughed.

Three Sunday Nights in February

When I was ten years old, I took a stand one Sunday night.

A spontaneous, yet justifiable (in my mind) "Why?" question came rolling right off of my tongue. It was directed toward my Daddy as we pulled into the church's parking lot.

"Why do I have to go to church on Sunday night if YOU don't?"

All I wanted to do was stay home and watch *Lassie* and *The Ed Sullivan Show* like Daddy, Mama and my baby brother were doing.

There was no response.

Nothing.

Not a word.

Maybe I was the victim of selective hearing?

Regardless, my plea apparently fell on deaf ears.

As usual, he dropped me off at the door of The First Baptist Church of Chamblee. I went in and did the weekly routine, Junior Choir practice with Dot Curtis, then children's Bible study with W. O. Brannan (the church called it "Training Union"). We ate a snack supper and then I came out and waited for Daddy. While I did enjoy all of the activities, I would've rather been home with my family watching Lassie and Ed Sullivan.

When I came out to look for Dad's car, something was different.

I saw our car.

It was parked.

Daddy was outside the door waiting for me with Mama and my younger brother, Phil.

Together, we went to the Sunday night worship service.

Hmmm, we'd never been to a Sunday night worship service as I recalled. It just turned out to be a casual version of the Sunday morning worship service with about half as many people there. It wasn't too bad. I was with my family, but the service sure wasn't *Lassie* or *The Ed Sullivan Show*.

My plea hadn't fallen on deaf ears at all.

Daddy just didn't have a good answer.

Either I wasn't going to have to go to church on Sunday night ... or they were.

My bluff was called ... I folded.

Together they decided they would come and go with me to church.

Allow me to elaborate. When I say, "Together they decided they would come and go with me to church," what I really mean is that Daddy had set his jaw firmly and now, "come hell or high water," we would regularly attend church on Sunday night.

He's a man of strong discipline.

Mama was pleased.

Heck, I never saw a Super Bowl until I went to college.

Youth choir, Training Union and the Sunday night service became a large part of my life. I made lots of good friends. We had tons of fun. Throughout my teen years it was the center of my social life.

We never missed church on Sunday night. Except ... for three consecutive Sundays in February of 1964.

The Beatles made their American debut on *The Ed Sullivan Show* on Sunday night, February 9, 1964. They were signed to perform on the show for three weeks. We watched them all. I don't know why we stayed home and watched the boys from Liverpool and the screaming throngs.

I never asked.

Whatever the reason, from someone's perspective it was important ... we were going to miss three straight Sunday night services. I suspect Mama had something to do with it.

Mama was an elementary school principal. She understood a lot about how the mind of a twelve-year-old boy functioned. Mama has always had a sixth sense about things, an open mind and a healthy willingness to embrace change. She was and remains wise beyond her years.

Could she have seen such a variance in the arts coming and know the cultural value of witnessing such an event for an impressionable child?

No doubt she could have.

As firmly set as Dad's jaw was once a decision was made, it somehow loosened. Daddy has always trusted Mama's instincts.

However ... maybe they, along with the rest of our parents, were just curious?

Entertainment had become predictable.

Maybe they were hoping for change that they could embrace?

Forty years removed from the "Roaring Twenties," the most marketable alternative to date was ... Elvis.

Maybe that's why The Beatles and their initiation of the "British Invasion" were such a prospective big deal in 1964. Who knows?

We all watched the television together. I remember my parents smiling, really trying to understand.

John, Paul, George, and Ringo ... the "Fab Four," strumming their electric guitars, shaking their "mops" of hair with bangs bouncing freely, their lack of nervousness in front of millions of viewers ... were clearly having fun.

Their music, while not yet revolutionary as it would become, was indeed fun.

"All My Loving," "Till There Was You," "She Loves You (Yeah, Yeah, Yeah)," "I Saw Her Standing There," and "I Wanna Hold Your Hand" were the songs on the first show.

And revolutionary or not, four of the five songs performed would be number one hits in 1964.

Regardless, of the relatively simple music and lyrics that we would hear over the next three Sunday nights, a line was drawn in the sand for the history of music. A line was drawn in the sand for the history of style.

Few of our parents understood what had taken place over these three Sunday nights in February. Most didn't try. Most didn't understand the impact this month had on their children. If you were too young to remember or hadn't been born, it's impossible to explain how much of the impact was immediately felt across the country and how spontaneously the change occurred.

It happened overnight.

Suddenly, on the morning of Monday, February 10, 1964, the great majority of young American high school boys threw away their tubes of Brylcreem hair ointment ... including me.

Seeking counsel from no one, I showered that morning and just combed through my hair, letting it dry and fall forward instead of "slicking" it back as I had before. When I arrived at school, hundreds of others had done the same. It was the same in every town across the country.

Over the next few weeks the new music and style shifts were on an unstoppable pace.

When we finally returned to the Sunday night service at church on the first weekend of March in 1964, there were bangs and dry hair everywhere.

We weren't the only ones who'd stayed home ... even some of the adults weren't using Brylcreem anymore.

Sleepless in Atlanta

Well, I can't sleep.

I'm up in the middle of the night, wide-awake like a kid waiting for Santa with an innocent childlike excitement. I'm awake and out of bed with visions of Major League Baseball playoffs dancing around in my head.

I love baseball.

It's October 2009 and the World Series is right around the corner and my team is in the hunt for the playoffs.

For crying out loud, I'm fifty-seven years old and dreaming about baseball. It's a problem that I've had for fifty years.

It was 1959, the year when Duke Snider and the Dodgers beat Nellie Fox and the White Sox in the World Series. We had a black and white television until the Dodgers won the pennant. I'll never forget my Daddy working two jobs so he would be able to afford a color television. He really wanted to watch the Series in color. Color television in 1959 was as high tech as it got. Today, I'm pretty sure I understand why he worked so hard to be able to watch the Series in color. I think Daddy just wanted to revisit the days of his youth when he sat in the stands at Ebbets Field as a kid and watched his Dodgers in person. Seeing the green grass, the red dirt infield, and the sea of Dodger blue uniforms on the television would make the game all the more special, bringing back childhood memories. Having grown up in New Haven, Connecticut, he was a lifelong Dodgers fan. Even though the team had departed Brooklyn the prior year and moved west to Los Angeles, they were still his team. He was as excited as a kid when they won that year. Heck, he was only thirty-four; he was still a kid.

Mickey Mantle was my childhood. Since the Yankees and Mickey weren't playing in the Series, I enthusiastically cheered for Dad's Dodgers as they beat the White Sox to win the 1959 Series, too.

I love baseball.

A couple years later, I walked all over the neighborhood checking for the best radio reception and finally came to rest, leaning against a pine tree in my next door neighbor's back yard. With a transistor radio pressed to my ear, I listened as Tracy Stallard faced Roger Maris on his second at-bat of the game. What kid that grew up loving baseball in the fifties couldn't tell you where they were that Sunday afternoon in October 1961 when Stallard delivered the pitch to Maris. I heard the crack of the bat and the roar of the crowd as the ball went into the right field stands of Yankee Stadium. Maris had hit his sixty-first home run of the season, breaking Babe Ruth's thirty-four-year-old record.

The crack of his bat still echoes in my memories.

I love baseball.

Have you ever read W. P. Kinsella's novel *Shoeless Joe*, or seen the movie *Field of Dreams*, based on his novel? Well, they ain't got a thing on my own childhood imagination. Ghosts walking out of a cornfield can't compare to the All-Stars running around my back yard. In my mind, Ted Williams, Willie Mays, Stan Musial, Hank Aaron, and my favorite, Mickey Mantle, were all playing there with me on our sand lot field.

Ah, baseball … a chess match of strategy played out on a baseball diamond. No lead is ever insurmountable. You can't run out of time; each team gets twenty-seven outs and your team can always have the chance to regain the lead no matter how far behind they are. The game, to quote Yogi Berra, "Ain't over 'til it's over!" All the statistics are a mathematician's dream … I can quote them in my sleep (which of course is one of the reasons why I'm awake … numbers, probability, statistics go on and on)!

Baseball truly was the national pastime for my childhood friends. Heck, I never even touched a football until I took the practice field in high school. Baseball was my life. Nothing was too farfetched for our gang. We all knew where to find one another. If you wanted to play baseball, which was every day for me, you just grabbed your glove and went to wherever you heard a crack of the bat and took a position in the field. There was always someone tossing a ball into the air and hitting it. All the neighborhood boys gathered on a vacant lot every day, rain or shine, and did their best to get a team together. Sometimes there were only a half dozen or so, but we played all the same. I would even play baseball all by myself if I found myself alone at the sand lot. Nothing except lightning and sometimes Mama stopped me.

I knew every big league starting player. The way they stood in the batter's box. The way they ran. The way they played the field. I studied the game with a passionate devotion and "became" my favorite players as I imitated their style on the field in my daily game.

Tonight, my sleep was interrupted by vivid memories rekindled in my dreams.

In 1966, my hometown finally got a Major League team. A group of businessmen lured the Milwaukee Braves to Atlanta. God bless every one of them.

It was unbelievable to finally have a hometown Major League team to call my own. And while I still rooted for Mickey Mantle until his playing days were over a few short years later, I have bled red-and-blue tomahawks with the Braves every season for the past forty-three years. Eddie Mathews, Hank Aaron, Joe Torre, Phil Niekro, Dale Murphy, Bob Horner, Bobby Cox, David Justice, Ron Gant, Tom Glavine, John Smoltz, Greg Maddux, Leo Mazzone, Chipper Jones, Andruw Jones, Brian McCann, and all of the others. They are my team; I am their fan. I will always be their fan.

Tonight, the reason I'm sleepless in Atlanta is that my team is only two games out in the wild card race and only four games out of the division lead with just six games to play. Are the Braves out of the race? Nope ... this year, 2009, they have never been more in it!

Win or lose, I love my team. I love the game.

To borrow a line from my Daddy's old Brooklyn Dodgers' faithful, "Wait 'til next year!"

Ah yes, I love baseball ... put on a pot of coffee, no sleep for me tonight!

The Box Cutter Made Me Do It

In the first grade, I took a little toy from my teacher's desk that didn't belong to me. She had collected the toy from a child who had brought it to school to enjoy, which was against the rules. Yep, I stole it. I kept it and played with it for several days, but I never enjoyed playing with the toy. Finally, I threw the toy away. I couldn't live with the guilt.

I have regretted stealing that toy from Mrs. Burris's desk my entire life.

The day that I celebrated my tenth birthday, I had an epiphany. Having completed the first ten years of my life, I reflected upon the length of a decade in the eyes of a newly added member of the club. I remember such musings as ... if I unexpectedly died in 1962 it could be etched on my headstone, "He lived a decade." I felt so old, mature, and accomplished. I'd lived long enough to see Roger Maris break Babe Ruth's single-season home run record. What else would ever top that?

Later during my old, mature, and accomplished tenth year, walking into the local drug store with my mother, I encountered a classmate named Lauren. Lauren spoke to me. I was horrified. She just smiled and kindly said, "Hi Dave." My Mom actually witnessed a girl attempting to exchange conversation with her firstborn male child. Mom had witnessed my first frightful attempt to exchange pleasantries with a girl in her presence.

All that I was able to utter to Lauren was, "Shut up." With those two words in my prepubescent opinion, I went from old, mature, and accomplished ... to rude, silly, and immature.

God bless her, Lauren must've been so embarrassed. Mom never mentioned it. Surely she was embarrassed as well. Instantaneously, I wished that I hadn't said it. I still do.

When I was sixteen I got my first job. I was a bag boy at the Big Apple grocery store in the Georgetown Shopping Center in Chamblee, Georgia. I sacked groceries for $1.55 an hour plus tips. I loved my job. Like my Daddy, I loved to work. As I extended my tenure of employment, my responsibilities increased to include mopping, incinerating cardboard boxes, and stocking the shelves with groceries. One of the benefits that accompanied the added responsibility of stocking the shelves was being presented with my own personal box cutter.

The box cutter made me do it.

Dr. Earl Craig was our pastor at The First Baptist Church of Chamblee. We were active members and I sang in the youth choir. I growled out the bass part to most of the songs the choir sang.

Every month or two after the Sunday night service we would have a baptism service. Baptist doctrine says that baptism must be done by immersion. The church had a small three or four foot deep indoor pool in the front of the choir loft. Each time Dr. Craig was going to do a baptism service, the congregation would sing a few songs while the baptism committee would assist those being baptized with undressing and putting on robes for the event. After removing his suit coat, Earl remained dressed in his suit and simply stepped into a pair of fishing waders that came up under his arms and kept him from getting wet during the event. A white robe covered Earl's tan waders from the congregation's sight ... it was a pastor's trade secret I never knew about as a younger child. By remaining dressed, Earl could slip out of the waders quickly enough to get to the back of the church to bid good wishes to the congregation as they departed.

I'm telling you, the box cutter made me do it.

Youth choir always met to practice in the afternoon before a period called Training Union. Baptist Training Union consisted of a series of courses that taught us about where the Bible stories we heard in Sunday school had originated. I know where each of the thirty-nine books of the Old Testament and the twenty-seven books of the New Testament in the Bible are located because of Training Union. Following Training Union there was a regular evening service of worship and occasionally, a baptism service followed.

One Sunday night, youth choir was excused from practice early. Having been recently entrusted with my box cutter from the grocery store, I never left home without it. I couldn't wait to show my new badge of honor to one of my best friends and fellow youth choir bass, Tandy Brannan. Throughout my life I've heard that "idle time is the devil's workshop" and this early dismissal from choir was to prove no exception. While we were waiting for Training Union to start, Tandy and I snooped around and found Earl's waders hanging unguarded in a closet under the choir loft. As Tandy watched the door, I whipped out my trusty new box cutter and with five or six quick slices I cut completely through the bottoms of the feet sections of the waders.

I don't remember how many people Earl baptized that night. I can tell you that it took four grown men to pull Earl out of the baptismal pool after his waders slowly filled up with water. You should have heard them laughing and trying not to get wet as they pulled him out of the pool. Earl was laughing the hardest of them all. Watching from the church balcony, Tandy and I gloated at the success of our practical joke.

Little did I know that Earl would eventually exact his revenge for our silly prank.

Six years later ... at the rehearsal dinner of my wedding, people who loved me stood and told stories about many of my more colorful childhood escapades. Earl, as the pastor who would marry us, was of course in attendance. Having known me most of my life, Earl stood to share a story along with the others. To my complete shock and embarrassment he told the entire wedding party about the time someone had sliced up the feet of his waders, that it was indeed my box cutter; and how I had nearly drowned him in the baptismal pool six years prior.

He knew I had done it and said nothing. He'd kept the secret for six years and waited until just the right moment for his revenge and I had a sick feeling he wasn't finished yet.

When I saw Earl the morning of our wedding, he assured me that we could let bygones be bygones and have a wonderful day together. Earl suggested that I leave the clothes that I would be wearing when we left for our honeymoon in his office to keep any pranksters at bay. I had a whole lot of friends that were practical jokers, so it seemed like a prudent idea to me.

It was a cold and bright December day at our beloved childhood church. Following the ceremony, our guests joined us in the fellowship hall for our reception. Earl joined us in the receiving line as was the tradition. We were greeting our guests and thanking them for celebrating our special day when there was a commotion of sorts in the parking lot. The local police were having some sort of emergency. With lights flashing and sirens blaring, multiple police cars arrived in the parking lot and several officers left their cars and headed toward the reception hall. The closer they came the more I wondered what could possibly have happened.

Earl left the reception line and went to meet the officers in what I was sure was an attempt to find out what was happening. Then I saw Earl motion toward me and I got a sinking feeling in the pit of my stomach. Uh-oh. The police officers were coming for me!

Earl had arranged for my "arrest." The charge ... "attempted drowning." With sirens blaring, the officers paraded me all through town before depositing me back at the reception. The people who attended the wedding had a memory likely to never be duplicated and Earl had his sweet revenge.

At last we were even. The crowd had a great laugh at my expense and Earl had proved he was every bit as good at playing a practical joke as he was at taking one. Don't dish it out if you can't take it. I figured I had it coming.

I ran off to Earl's office to change clothes and prepare to meet my bride at the car where we would be likely covered in rice before our departure. As I reached for my shirt and pants I realized Earl had one last laugh on me ... both had been soaking in a bucket of ice water.

Touché.

As I left the church to make the drive to the airport in a soaking wet suit, Earl smiled as he simply said, "We're even." I humbly accepted his offer of a truce.

Regrets ... yep, I've had a few.

I wish that I could tell Mrs. Burris how sorry I was for stealing the toy.

I wish that I could find Lauren and apologize to her for being so childishly rude.

Do I regret slicing the bottom out of my pastor Earl's waders?

Nah ... Some things just aren't that regrettable.

A Humble Wagon, A Haunting Song

It's been over forty-three years and I've never told a soul until today.

Tommy and I went together.

School was cancelled on Tuesday.

I was in the tenth grade at Chamblee High School in Chamblee, Georgia, a suburb of Atlanta.

Looking for something to do since school was cancelled, I decided to walk over to my old neighbor's house that morning and see if I could hang out with him the rest of the day.

Tommy was my next-door neighbor from 1956 until we moved about a mile away in 1965. We were the same age. He was my best friend.

It was April 9, 1968.

The previous Thursday, Martin Luther King, Jr. was assassinated in Memphis, Tennessee. He was a native of Atlanta. Tuesday was the day of his funeral. Schools were closed as a sign of respect for the slain leader of the civil rights movement.

Tommy and I sat outside on the porch and talked about Dr. King's death. As we talked, we remembered the November day in 1963 when President Kennedy was killed.

We were classmates in Miss Sutton's sixth grade class when our school principal, H.O. Cravey, made the announcement about the President, his voice breaking as it came over the intercom telling us the news. Miss Sutton openly wept.

We usually walked home from school. Not that day.

Tommy's mother, Betty, picked us up from school. When we saw her waiting for us in her car, even at such a young age we understood that she felt the same shock and grief we'd witnessed before we left our class. Betty was the happiest person in any of our lives, but that afternoon she was solemn. She didn't know if we knew the President was dead. She couldn't tell us without tears.

I was moved.

Tommy and I remembered. We remembered it all.

During the next passing days, families everywhere across the world sat together and watched on the television as the funeral procession came through the capital. I watched the President's funeral with Tommy.

We saw the six gray horses as they pulled the flag-draped casket on a gleaming wagon that shone in the midday sun. We remembered the black stallion following the casket with no rider and the boots placed backwards in the saddle's stirrups. We watched as the President's son, "John-John," spun and saluted his father one last time.

As we remembered the events of almost five years before, we pondered the funeral arrangements for Dr. King.

We had heard no mention of the funeral being televised. We knew that the funeral would be through the streets of downtown Atlanta.

Those were the days of going to play outside and not coming home until dark. There were never any questions about where you'd been or what you'd done. Most days involved a baseball game.

It was nothing for us to get on the bus and ride downtown to a Braves game. We could get in for a buck and sit in the upper deck. We'd ridden downtown to the Municipal Auditorium for afternoon rock concerts and their funny smells. The bus ride cost a dime. We'd ridden the bus all over town.

Spontaneously, we decided to take the bus and attend the funeral procession. We walked to the bus stop near Oglethorpe University, paid the bus driver the fare and began the thirty-minute ride to downtown Atlanta.

We walked along the processional route and found a place along with several thousand other people who were waiting to pay their respects to the fallen leader. It was a quiet and reverent wait for the procession.

We had no idea of the significance of the event we were about to witness.

We waited.

And ... we waited.

Then, in the distance, we heard singing.

As the song neared our position, others near us began to sing along.

"We shall overcome ... we shall overcome some day." Tommy and I weren't familiar with the words or the tune they were singing. *"Oh deep in my heart, I do believe that we shall overcome some day."* The song's words were penetrating both of our hearts.

We listened.

This was the most solemn moment that I ever witnessed in person, thousands of people respectfully honoring a life given for such a noble cause.

And then I saw it.

Two mules were pulling a very old, humble, roughhewn buckboard wagon that contained the casket of Dr. King. As it passed us, the clack, clack, clack of the metal rims on the wooden spoke wheels slowly kept time with the rhythm of the song.

A humble buckboard wagon would carry him home to his final resting place.

From our memory together of watching a presidential funeral five years before, with all of the appropriate grand and elegant process required for a head of state, to personally witnessing this most humble gesture of a great leader being carried in a humble wagon, Tommy and I were overwhelmed.

Tears stained our faces from the grief we felt.

As tens of thousands of people walked passed us, Tommy and I just stood and respectfully waited for the procession.

When they had passed, he asked me if I had seen Jackie Kennedy walking with the people. I said no.

All I remember seeing was a humble wagon carrying this visionary proponent for non-violent change to his grave.

Tommy said we should catch the bus home. He was probably right.

Yet ... I hesitated.

As we turned to go, I told him I wanted to walk with the people in the funeral procession for a while. Tommy wanted to go home.

We talked about the concern for safety if we separated. Being alone in the city was something that we'd never done before. Tommy wondered aloud if we should have come at all ... I told him that right or wrong we came, and that nothing was going to change the fact that we'd been there.

He relaxed and said he was glad we came.

The crowd was characterized by a deep sincerity. We believed we would be safe. We decided that it would be okay to continue alone.

Nonetheless, Tommy's inner instinct told him it would be best if we just kept the events of this afternoon between us.

He asked me to "swear to God" that I would keep it between us. Now, you have to understand, "swearing to God" was the highest promise a kid who went to church every Sunday could make. Tommy and I were regulars in the Methodist and Baptist churches in Chamblee.

I said I would swear it in my heart.

He asked me to say it out loud.

I relented.

I swore ... out loud.

We parted.

I hurriedly joined in the very back of the funeral procession.

I stretched to see the buckboard wagon again. It was nowhere to be seen.

I walked alone in the crowd until we reached Dr. King's alma mater, Morehouse College, just west of downtown. A public funeral service was to be held on the campus.

There, after it had come to a stop ... I took one last glimpse at the old humble wagon.

I could leave now.

I was one of several hundred participants who were returning to town after the conclusion of the march to the Morehouse campus. As we walked together, the crowd was silent until a gentleman in front of me with a rich bass voice quietly began to sing the now familiar song, *"We shall overcome ..."* As he finished his lone solo verse the masses began to sing again. *"We shall live in peace ..."*

I joined along.

On the bus ride home, the day, the wagon, and the song never left my mind.

Over forty years later, the day, the wagon, and the song still echo in my thoughts.

I lost my old friend Tommy to a tragic accident over twenty years ago.

I've never told a soul about our day together on April 9, 1968, until today.

I really don't even know why he didn't think he wanted to tell anybody.

But, I swore.

I've told the story of going to the funeral before. I've always wanted to include the person who really went with me.

But, I swore to God I wouldn't tell.

I never would have gone alone. I've even made up that another person went with me to protect Tommy's request.

He made me swear out loud!

People could hear me "swear to God."

I'll never do any "swearing to God" again.

If it hadn't been for Tommy ... shoot, I would have ended up kicking cans all day.

Recently, I had a compulsion to write the story of the humble wagon.

Well, I couldn't write the story down and mention that I went by myself when I didn't. And I dang sure wasn't going to give credit to somebody else for going with me who wasn't with me. I wasn't going to rest until I wrote it down, so ... I asked God earlier if it would be okay to tell you, but I haven't heard anything yet.

Therefore ... I went to the person I consider God's closest ally, my Mama.

I had breakfast with my eighty-seven-year-old Mama and told her the story this morning.

She'd known for years that I went to the funeral; I told her myself for crying out loud. However, I'd never mentioned Tommy. I asked if she thought it would be okay for me to tell our story.

Mama is objective. She'll know how to handle it. She was an elementary school principal years ago. She said Tommy probably didn't want his Mama and Daddy getting upset with him for being downtown all day, leaving me alone and coming home by himself.

That's it?

She then gently reminded me that Tommy, his Mama and Daddy have all died. It was her opinion that telling the story would be okay. I knew she'd know what to do.

My life was forever altered that afternoon with my friend, the humble wagon, and the haunting song.

"The Tie that Binds"

"Men are what their mothers made them."
~ Ralph Waldo Emerson

In an unforeseen change of events, the most wonderful thing happened. I got to spend a year getting to know and love my Mama all over again. Mama was eighty. I was moving back to Atlanta and I couldn't wait.

I planned to rent a place somewhere in town temporarily until it was determined where I would permanently settle. Atlanta has so many options. Would I choose a downtown loft, a midtown condo, a Buckhead high rise, a house in the suburbs, a place on the lake, or maybe even a cozy cabin in the mountains of Big Canoe, who knew? While looking for temporary housing, I stayed with Mom and Dad in their guest room over their garage. It was a nice sized room with a private bath and at their insistence, it quickly became the temporary housing I was seeking.

A chance to be back close to my folks . . . Mom's cooking, watching every imaginable sporting event with Dad, their interactions with one another, our fellowship together. Time to get to know them all over again, this time not as a child. What a privilege. We sure had fun.

I spent a year with my folks before I was ready to leave. It was one of the most important years of my life. During that year, my workdays began at 6:00 a.m. and concluded at 9:00 p.m., fifteen hours a day, Monday through Friday. I searched Atlanta for housing on the weekends.

Dad and I left for work about the same time early each morning. He has been a greeter at Wal-Mart for the past twenty years. He loves to work. He longs for the fellowship. The responsibilities beckon him. He is happiest when he feels productive. By the time I got home from work every night, he was already in bed. He needed his rest. During my time with them I really only saw Dad on the weekends. Mama, however, was always waiting on me when I arrived home every night.

I really got to know my Mama during our year together. I quietly observed her in her element. Her thoughts. Her actions. Her habits. Her character. I learned how much my Mama cares ... about everyone.

Lemme tell you a few things about my Mama.

Mama loves the Lord.

During a revival meeting when she was a child, as the congregation sang, *"I will arise and go to Jesus,"* she did. Her decision was profound and through the years, she has followed Jesus. She has been a member of Friendship Baptist Church, First Baptist Church of Chamblee, and is currently a member of First Baptist Church of Roswell, Georgia. She has always loved the church.

Mama cares about the Lord's work.

Every night when I came home, Mama was always up, busy doing something for somebody. Something for Daddy, anyone in our family, anyone in their church, any of their friends (past or present), "the needy" ... there was always someone that Mama needed to help. Her endless nightly activities were always productive.

There was always a meal for me whenever I arrived home, even when I suggested that she shouldn't go to the trouble. When I finished eating, she would never let me help her clean up the dishes. All she wished for was to have me talk to her while she did the work.

Mama cares.

Lord . . . how my Mama loves my Daddy. Every night she would set the kitchen table with placemats and cloth napkins; when he awoke early for work he could just sit down and have a nice breakfast of cereal, fruit and such. It wasn't uncommon for her to have an article she thought he would enjoy reading beside his plate. Every night she packed Daddy a lunch for the following day. I bet I saw her put peanut butter on a thousand saltine crackers while I was there. He likes 'em that way.

She loves my Daddy so much.

Mama loves each one of us.

"The Tie that Binds"

In our house, Mama has always said she has three "boys"—Dad, my brother, and me. She calls us her three little pigs (or in her affectionate voice, her three little "pids").

Now that we are grown, our families are the first recipients of her love. She is the glue that has held our family together for decades. We would not be the individuals or the family we are without her wit, wisdom, teaching, and devotion. If she loves you . . . you are truly and deeply loved. Once her love has a hold on you, it will never let go. There are no conditions to her love. None.

Oh how she loves her family.

Mama communicates.

Mama really knows how to use the telephone. She calls countless relatives to check on them, find out how they are doing, get the latest news, and see if they need anything. If she can't reach them on the phone, she does it either the new or old-fashioned way. Heck, Mama, who was eighty-seven in June, will send someone a text message or an e-mail in a skinny minute and if she doesn't hear from them pretty soon, she will sit right down and write them a letter.

Her childhood friends consisted primarily of the thirty-five first cousins on her Daddy's side, the Tribble family. The great majority of their homes were within walking distance of each other. Only four cousins remain—her brother, L. H. (ninety), Mama and Dorothy (each of them eighty-seven), and Thad (the youngest, who is eighty). She used to rely on her cousins to keep her informed as to the well-being of their children. Now, she has to depend on the children themselves. She formed the "Tribble Family Reunion" to sustain the family ties that bind us together.

Mama cares for every member of her family.

Mama is a social butterfly. She has innumerable friends and is always looking to make new ones. If you have ever been her friend, you will always be her friend. She's gonna treat you the same as family regardless of your circumstances. She is a source of endless encouragement.

Mama is a loyal and beloved friend.

Mama bakes cakes.

Any occasion is a signal for Mama to bake a cake. Anything that affects anyone she knows sounds an internal caring alarm that calls her into action. Any occasion. Birth. Death. Sickness. Health. Sadness. Happiness. Arrival. Departure. A leaf falls from a newly planted tree. A little leaguer gets a base hit. Any occasion. Everyone LOVES getting one of Mama's cakes. One night during my year with Mama, I asked her how many cakes she made in an average year. She pondered for a moment and said, "About seventy-five." Seventy-five cakes a year for the last sixty years . . . well, you do the math. She's baked somewhere between 4,000 and 5,000 homemade cakes . . . over 50,000 pieces of cake! Each one delivered in a new white cake box tied with a ribbon and a bow. Without any fanfare, while maintaining a low profile, she gives her best to others and remains faithful to her mission of delivering love along with her wonderful cakes. Cakes are Mama's calling. They are her best expression of caring about folks.

Mama cares. She bakes cakes.

If Mama knows it's happening, she will always come. Mama is always there.

Every time the door of the church is open. Baby showers. Bridal showers. Births. Bridal luncheons. Weddings. Music recitals. Dance recitals. Basketball games. Retirements. Baseball games. Football games. Soccer games. Beauty contests. Graduations. Funerals. Funerals. Funerals.

Mama cares. She is always there. She understands the incalculable value of a person's presence.

Mama has style and she loves a bargain.

She is as apt to wear a pair of red shoes today as she was sixty years ago. She likes her house to be decorated with a flair that is her own. She has a good eye for design and her taste is beyond compare.

At 4:00 a.m. on "Black Friday" during my year with her, Mama dragged me out of bed on a cold, rainy morning to get to Value City so that she could buy four Waterford crystal water glasses that matched her crystal pattern for only $24.99 each. It was a big savings! She already had twelve stems of the crystal and she explained that if she had four more, she could leave my brother and me enough for each of us to have service for eight some day in the future ... naturally, all sixteen will have been well used. Her Mother, my Granny Tribble, was content to drink out of "jelly jars" as she and PaPa did most of the time, but not Mama. She wanted the best for us. As I watched her literally run from my truck in the pouring rain to secure her place in line that cold morning, I couldn't help but laugh out loud at what Granny would think of her eighty-year-old daughter running through a cold, wet parking lot at 4:00 in the morning just to get a bargain on glasses that cost $24.99 each. If she were still alive Granny would just shake her head and grin as she said, "I am satisfied that she needed them."

Mama cares about making things nice. She loves a deal on something she wants. She always makes everything "just right" . . . she has "the knack."

Mama has a great sense of humor.

Mama loves to laugh! It is so much fun to listen as she attempts to tell a joke. She often gets tickled at herself as she tells a story; it isn't unusual halfway through for her to snort, snicker, and have her eyes fill with tears at the hilarity of the approaching punch line. Many times watching her storytelling is as much fun as her story. Mama loves for everyone to have fun. She just loves to see people laughing and happy.

Mama cares about smiles, laughter, and fun.

Spending a year with Mama and Daddy opened my eyes to their happiness with one another. In August they celebrated their sixtieth wedding anniversary. Oh, they bark every now and then like "Archie and Edith," but honestly, they are just as cute as buttons together. They still seem to be "googly-eyed" over each other. Dad insists they both just need stronger bifocals . . .

In my year with them, I saw her invaluable contributions to so many people's lives. I'm so glad it took a year to find the right home for myself. Of course, she played a part in helping me find it. We wandered all over Atlanta on the weekends looking for the opportunities that were available. I valued her opinion. Mama has the knack. After considering many places, I decided that my best choice was a cozy cabin in the mountains of Big Canoe. After having taken the time get to know me better than ever, Mama liked the cozy cabin best for me, too.

Mama cares about me.

Mama loves the Lord. Mama loves my Daddy. Mama loves her sons and their families. Mama loves her church. Mama loves all of her family. Mama loves her friends.

Born of humble beginnings, hers is a life dedicated to service. My Mama, Helen Grace Tribble Brown, is an amazing human being.

No person has had a greater influence on me than Mama. As the old gospel song so wisely suggests, *"Blest be the tie that binds."* Mama is my family's *"tie that binds."* And because she cares, all of those she has touched throughout her life also care.

Each of us cares more because she cares.

It was so much fun spending that year with Mama. Right smack in the middle of my life I was given the privilege of spending a year with my parents. It was so much fun.

And the fun goes on.

An Extraordinary, Ordinary Man

My first memory of being in church is standing on the pew beside Mama, my jaw protruding like my Daddy's, concentrating on the two men in the baptistry.

The two of them stood together in the concrete block baptismal pool of the old white clapboard building that was The First Baptist Church of Chamblee. It was 1956. Both men stood erect, jaws jutting forward with a bulldog bravado that came from the inherited underbites of their parents. These were serious men and this was a serious moment.

Our Pastor, Cecil Sherman, was a twenty-nine-year-old "Soldier of The Cross." His calling led him from his home in Texas to our church in Chamblee, Georgia. He and his wife, Dot joined our church the same Sunday in September as Mama, Daddy, and me.

My Daddy, Lee Brown, was originally from New Haven, Connecticut. Daddy was a thirty-one-year-old veteran of World War II. He served as a United States Army Ranger. After surviving D-Day's first wave of the Omaha Beach landing at Normandy twelve short years prior, as well as the remainder of the war, he moved south to Georgia. He had fallen in love, married my Mama, and they started a family.

On this day Daddy was professing his faith in Christ by presenting himself for baptism. With his right hand on my father's back, Cecil lowered Daddy into the baptismal waters and raised him from them, symbolizing his inclusion in the body of faith.

Their jaws were set. Their hearts forever bound.

As Daddy was raised from the waters, our family's commitment to Christ was cemented. Our family would be consistent in our support of Christ's church. During times of adversity in my life I have come to rely on the spiritual safe haven of the great hymns of the church. Based on scripture, sung with a repetitive and memorable tune, the words from the hymns of my childhood have resounded throughout my life as a fortress against any trouble that might come along. Today at age fifty-eight, I am thankful for the privilege my parents extended to me from the discipline of regularly attending church. The frequency of repeating the scripture through the stanzas of the hymns and committing them to memory as a child has granted me more strength and inner peace in my life than I would have ever imagined possible.

Cecil and Daddy's loyalty to one another remained steadfast though many miles would soon separate them. There would be more children (my brother, Phil, and Cecil and Dot's daughter, Eugenia "Genie," were born the next year), more education, and varied positions of leadership as their careers evolved. Both men had taken stands for freedom, Daddy as a patriot and Cecil in his role as a pastor. They were always loyal to one another, their loyalty always revolving around their shared unspoken passion for freedom. The respect and appreciation they shared for one another and each other's family never wavered.

Cecil was with us in Chamblee for four short years before he and his family moved back to Texas and then to Asheville, North Carolina where he was the pastor of The First Baptist Church of Asheville for twenty years.

Many years prior to his move to Asheville and two years prior to Cecil's arrival in Chamblee, our church founded a summer camp for the youth of the church. During Cecil's tenure in Chamblee he had a great impact on the development of the camp and its ministry. First, Camp Daniel Morgan—later Camp Rutledge—was held at a Georgia State Park about an hour east of Atlanta. Each year, our youth attended camp for a week during the middle of July. Youth Camp (ages thirteen through seventeen) was held the first week and then Junior Camp (ages nine through twelve) was held the following week.

During the time Cecil served in Asheville, his church attended camp with ours. It was here that I developed a personal relationship with Cecil, first as a camper and then as a camp counselor. As a camper, I recalled that he was a bold, serious, devout, no-nonsense kind of man. He had a job to do and he did it. He still had that bulldog jaw. As a counselor, I began to know him as a devoted family man with a quick wit, an encyclopedic mind, unmovable convictions, and a kind heart that loved all.

One weekend when I was a counselor at Camp Rutledge we had a free day before the Junior Campers were to arrive. A softball game was planned for all of the counselors late in the afternoon. Cecil was to be the coach of one of the teams. The camp director asked Cecil to call the coin toss to start our game. As the coin was flipped high into the air ... with a resounding conviction ringing across the field for all to hear, Cecil called, "Sides." Not "Heads" or "Tails" but "Sides." The coin landed against a blade of grass on its *side*. Cecil, as though he knew it would happen, turned and confidently declared, "We'll take the field." I was on Cecil's team that day.

Like my father before me, I've been on his team ever since.

Cecil's hand remained on our family for fifty more memorable years. From my first impression of Cecil as he baptized my Daddy, his continued involvement in my development as a young person, and his dedication as a noble leader in his denomination, I have never encountered a bolder example of leadership as he strived for freedom in Christ for everyone.

In my life I have recognized many different types of individuals. Three come to mind as I think of Cecil. First, dreamers. Second, doers. And third, those who are the most rare of all—those who willingly take a stand for their convictions. Cecil took multiple stands for his convictions while he served in Asheville. As Johnson Oatman's hymn *"Higher Ground"* says in the second stanza, *"My heart has no desire to stay, where doubts arise and fears dismay. Though some may dwell where these abound, my prayer, my aim is higher ground."* Cecil always stood on higher ground. Cecil stood against racism. Cecil stood for freedom in Christ within his own denomination. He refused to let *"fears dismay"* while he was in Asheville. Even though personally threatened, Cecil firmly stood on higher ground.

Cecil died this past Saturday.

His lion's heart, though finally quiet, roared for freedom one last time.

The echo of his roar will never be silenced.

Daddy ... My Hero

"Every man who set foot on Omaha Beach that day was a hero."
~ Lt. Gen. Omar N. Bradley, *Invasion Commander,*
U.S. ground forces, June 6, 1944

His smiles are more and more frequent and they are getting brighter as time goes by. It all began following his retirement nearly twenty years ago when Dad, just for the fun of it, chose to start another career. He spends four days a week greeting customers at Wal-Mart. He loves welcoming customers into the store. Wal-Mart loves Dad. He smiles all day.

He's eighty-six years old and is happy all of the time.

I've only seen Daddy cry three times in my life. Me? I cried three times yesterday.

Yesterday . . . tears first came to my eyes as I watched one of my old football coaches waddle down the aisle in church and slowly kneel at the altar. I watched as he tearfully prayed for his wife of fifty years who is battling cancer. Later, I was watching the end of the forty-year-old football movie *Brian's Song,* about Chicago Bears running back Brian Piccolo. Piccolo was dying of cancer. When Piccolo's roommate, Gayle Sayers, makes the last speech to the team on Brian's behalf, tears were streaking down my face. Last night, a native Canadian skier won the first gold medal ever in an Olympic event hosted in Canada. The winner's brother has cerebral palsy. The athlete's motivation came greatly from his handicapped brother's support; his brother is his biggest fan. He dedicated his medal to his brother. Overjoyed, they embraced at the finish line of the skier's triumph and I cried for the third time . . . yesterday.

Dad was the middle child of three. My "Granny Bim" raised them as a single parent during the Depression. Uncle Larry was five years older than Dad and they had a baby sister named Mary. Bim was a cleaning lady at Yale University in New Haven. Hard work came naturally for my Dad and his family.

Dad loves his country. Enough to unashamedly shed a tear for his loyalty. The three times I have seen him shed a tear, his patriotism was a part of the equation.

Uncle Larry joined the Army in the late 1930s. At eighteen, Dad followed his brother into World War II in the early 1940s as an Army Ranger.

They both saw extensive action in battle. They both made it home.

Uncle Larry made the Army his career. He retired after thirty years of service. Shortly after retiring, sadly he was diagnosed with a terminal form of cancer. In early 1972, Uncle Larry came to see us for the last time. He came to tell us goodbye. I was in college at Furman University and had come home for the weekend to see him for what would be the last time. It was hard to leave to return to school that night. Dad and Mom sensed that I understood that this would be the last time we would see him together and were slow to tell me to leave for my two-and-a-half-hour trip back to Furman. Uncle Larry could see what was happening and, always the Sergeant Major, barked out his final orders to me, "Why don't you get your ass back to school?" I hugged him . . . those were the last words I ever heard him say.

Sgt. Major H. H. "Larry" Brown was fifty-two years old when he died.

Within the shadow of our nation's Capital building, in Arlington National Cemetery with a full military burial, Uncle Larry's flag-draped casket was laid to rest alongside other fallen heroes in one of our country's most hallowed places. Our family was in the funeral procession's motorcade and I was seated next to Dad in the front seat of our car. As we came into view of the Army Military Honor Guard, tears began to roll down Dad's cheeks and he simply whispered, "Larry would be so proud." I was twenty years old and this was the first time I ever saw my Daddy cry.

During the war, Dad served in the infantry as an Army Ranger. His battalion landed in the first assault of Omaha Beach in Normandy, France on D-Day.

Dad never talked about the war.

Never.

After I finished at Furman, Dad and I worked together for a few years. On June 6, 1984, I happened to be in the office where a television was playing. People in the office were gathered to watch the fortieth anniversary commemoration of the D-Day invasion. About a dozen of us gathered to watch President Ronald Reagan deliver a speech commemorating the occasion. Dad eased into the very back of the room to take in Reagan's words.

We stand on a lonely, windswept point on the northern shore of France. The air is soft, but forty years ago at this moment, the air was dense with smoke and the cries of men, and the air was filled with the crack of rifle fire and the roar of cannon. At dawn, on the morning of the 6th of June 1944, two hundred and twenty-five Rangers jumped off the British landing craft and ran to the bottom of these cliffs. Their mission was one of the most difficult and daring of the invasion: to climb these sheer and desolate cliffs and take out the enemy guns. The Allies had been told that some of the mightiest of these guns were here, and they would be trained on the beaches to stop the Allied advance.

The Rangers looked up and saw the enemy soldiers -- at the edge of the cliffs shooting down at them with machine guns and throwing grenades. And the American Rangers began to climb. They shot rope ladders over the face of these cliffs and began to pull themselves up. When one Ranger fell, another would take his place. When one rope was cut, a Ranger would grab another and begin his climb again. They climbed, shot back, and held their footing. Soon, one by one, the Rangers pulled themselves over the top, and in seizing the firm land at the top of these cliffs, they began to seize back the continent of Europe. Two hundred and twenty-five came here. After two days of fighting, only ninety could still bear arms.

Behind me is a memorial that symbolizes the Ranger daggers that were thrust into the top of these cliffs. And before me are the men who put them there.

These are the boys of Pointe du Hoc. These are the men who took the cliffs. These are the champions who helped free a continent. These are the heroes who helped end a war.

Gentlemen, I look at you and I think of the words of Stephen Spender's poem. You are men who in your "lives fought for life ... and left the vivid air signed with your honor..."

Forty summers have passed since the battle that you fought here. You were young the day you took these cliffs; some of you were hardly more than boys, with the deepest joys of life before you. Yet you risked everything here. Why? Why did you do it? What impelled you to put aside the instinct for self-preservation and risk your lives to take these cliffs? What inspired all the men of the armies that met here? We look at you, and somehow we know the answer. It was faith, and belief; it was loyalty and love.

The men of Normandy had faith that what they were doing was right, faith that they fought for all humanity, faith that a just God would grant them mercy on this beachhead or on the next. It was the deep knowledge -- and pray God we have not lost it -- that there is a profound moral difference between the use of force for liberation and the use of force for conquest. You were here to liberate, not to conquer, and so you and those others did not doubt your cause. And you were right not to doubt.

You all knew that some things are worth dying for. One's country is worth dying for, and democracy is worth dying for, because it's the most deeply honorable form of government ever devised by man. All of you loved liberty. All of you were willing to fight tyranny, and you knew the people of your countries were behind you.

~ President Ronald Reagan, June 6, 1984

At the conclusion of Reagan's speech, our colleagues turned along with me to see my Dad standing by himself, hand over his heart, tears flowing down his cheeks for the men, his fellow Rangers that never came home from Normandy. I was thirty-two and this was the second time I'd seen Daddy cry.

During the summer of 2007, Dad had surgery for a knee replacement. There were complications following the surgery and he fell gravely ill with congestive heart failure. After enduring two heart attacks and spending two weeks in intensive care he became stable enough to attempt multiple bypass surgery. The procedure was successful and Dad was quickly on the mend. He was assigned to a rehabilitation facility where he would spend the next month overcoming both the knee and heart procedures.

Working in an office very near the rehabilitation center, it was very convenient to go by and see him on a regular basis. Dad is a great patient. He always sees the proverbial glass half full.

Every morning during the week I would go by McDonald's and get Dad and myself a cup of coffee. Most mornings I would arrive at the facility before he awoke. I would just wait for him to wake up and then we'd enjoy a cup of coffee together before he had to begin his treatments.

I usually didn't go to see him on the weekend. Yet one Saturday morning during his stay, I got out of bed and thought I'd surprise him with a cup of coffee ... McDonald's two sugars and cream, as usual. I arrived before he awoke. He was surprised and pleased that I would have gotten out of bed and come to have a cup of coffee with him on the weekend.

Still a little hazy from the previous night's sleep, he became quiet and said to me, "I had that dream again last night." Completely unfamiliar with him ever mentioning a recurrent dream, I simply inquired, "What dream is that, Dad?" He paused and said, "The one where all of the boys are dying on the beach and calling for their mothers." His lower lip began to quiver and tears filled and spilled from his eyes as he uttered, "They were all so young, so young." Over sixty years later and he still dreams about "boys dying on the beach and calling for their mothers." I was fifty-five.

At forty-seven, Dad lost a brother and fellow soldier to cancer.

At fifty-nine, he remembered fallen soldiers with which he fought to save the world.

At eighty-two, over sixty years after he was there, he still dreams of the horrors of war and the massive loss of young lives on Omaha Beach.

In August of 2009, sixty-five years after the D-Day invasion, the French government bestowed on him the highest honor of France, the French Legion of Honor Medal. Presented by the French Consul General on behalf of the French President, *"With appreciation of France to Sgt. Lee M. Brown, of Alpharetta, Georgia, a decorated World War II veteran of the U.S. Army 5th Ranger Battalion, for his valor on Omaha Beach during the D-Day landing, I award you France's highest honor."*

Thank you, France, for showing your honor, appreciation, and respect to my Dad for his bravery. Don't stop. Find every brave veteran that came to liberate your country from tyranny and pin a medal on every one of them.

Next week Dad, Mom and my brother will be a part of the American memorial celebration of the 67th anniversary of the D-Day invasion. Together they will walk the same route on Omaha Beach in Normandy that Dad and so many others crawled across as they sought to save the world from fascism. Dad is finally ready to return the place of his finest hour as an American. He wants to touch the waters of the Atlantic one last time and remember where his innocence was lost and he emerged as a warrior fighting for the cause of freedom. They will stand together at the top of Pointe du Hoc and remember all of the sacrifices made. Some medical issues prevent me from being with them; however, all four of our spirits will be gathered atop those cliffs together where a piece of each of our hearts will remain forever.

My Dad, Lee Brown, is an American hero.

He is my hero.

And . . . at eighty-six, Dad is all smiles.

Do-Be, Do-Be, Do

"To be is to do. ~ Socrates"
"To do is to be. ~ Plato"
"Do-Be, Do-Be, Do. ~ Sinatra"

~ Sam Yoshimura

What did I want to be when I got out of Furman?

I had just graduated from high school and suddenly everybody seemed to be curious as to what I wanted to be after I graduated from college.

Everyone seemed to press with questions and demands, "Tell me, tell me, TELL ME!"

Everyone knew the answer ... didn't they?

I thought the answer was obvious. When I finished college ... I wanted to be happy.

There, that's it.

What?

That's not what you meant.

OH, you mean what do I want to DO for a living when I finish college? You mean what kind of job do I want?

Heck, I don't have the first clue. Do I have to be in a hurry? Am I supposed to know what job I want at eighteen? Isn't that what college is for?

To this day, I've only ever known one person in my life who knew what they really wanted to do when he finished college even before he started. He was a classmate of mine at Furman named Greer. All he ever wanted to do was sell wholesale appliances back home in Georgia. He got a job doing exactly that and almost forty years later after moving a few rungs up the corporate ladder, he's still involved with selling appliances.

God bless him. How did he know? Incredible.

Now really, how in the world could I know what I wanted to do as I was just finishing high school? I was barely eighteen. Heck, I didn't even really figure out who I was before I was forty.

Up until I left for college at eighteen the only things I'd ever done were babysit, cut grass, play baseball and football, lifeguard, and sack groceries.

Do I choose from one of those? Are those the only choices I have?

Ain't no way I'm ever babysitting again unless it's for my own children or grandchildren. I'm allergic to grass, can't hit a curve ball, and I'm too small and too slow to make a living that has anything to do with football. Lifeguard, yeah right ... I haven't even been to Florida yet and I've only seen pictures of the ocean. And all the grocery stores are going do-it-yourself!

What? ... You're telling me I should have been observing people and considering what they do and have developed an interest in doing something similar by now? Is this written down somewhere? Did we discuss this in school when I was sick?

I should have been observing people, huh?

Fair enough.

I'll try to remember back through my first eighteen years.

Wow, my recollections are that most people seem miserable and can't wait for the weekend to come so they don't have to do their job anymore. Most people whine and gripe constantly about work. As a general rule, most adults I have observed don't appear to be happy. A lot of that seems to happen because of what they do.

Wait a minute.

I did remember one guy from my childhood who was always singing, whistling, always had a skip in his step and a twinkle in his eye. His name was Fred Kramer and he was our neighbor. If Fred liked you, he'd give you a nickname and never call you anything else. He called my brother "Casper the friendly ghost." Casper was a cartoon character whose head was shaped like a light bulb. When Phil had a crew cut in the summer he looked just like Casper. For me, he just adopted my long-time childhood nickname and called me "Crockett," as in *"the king of the wild frontier,"* Davy Crockett.

Fred loved kids. Every weekend, he gathered the neighborhood kids together and—appropriately clothed in his boxer shorts, t-shirt, and flip-flops—he would pitch, umpire, and broadcast our weekly neighborhood softball games in his backyard. We practiced all week just to be ready for our weekend game with Fred. His pitching was perfect. Every kid got a hit. He called balls and strikes just like a big league "ump" and broadcast our entire game sounding just like Dizzy Dean and Pee Wee Reese broadcasting the "Game of the Week." After the game he would sit down to enjoy his own special "home brew." You see, he liked to brew his own beer and he thoroughly enjoyed his homemade brew following our game. Fred would occasionally let us take a sip; I always thought it tasted like soapy-water. His son Mark and I became really good pals playing those games in his backyard every weekend. Man, we had fun.

Fred was happy.

Hmmm, I made a note of Fred for future reference. What did he do, you ask?

Fred was a salesman.

Let's get back to college and what I was going to learn to do so that I could be happy.

Why Furman University?

There are five simple reasons.

First, they teach you to love "learning" there.

Second, it was a small school and you got to know an entire community of students that was as diverse as the four winds.

Third, Furman was an academically challenging school and I needed to be challenged. I was bored the first twelve years I was in school. Everything came easily and I knew I could do better. I wanted to do better.

Fourth, I wanted a liberal arts education to help me appreciate the world and its cultures … an education that would challenge, yet keep me in synchronization with my Christian beliefs.

Note to reader: the first four reasons didn't count … they were *my* reasons.

Okay … fifth, my pastor, Dr. Earl Craig, went to school at Furman and my parents thought I wouldn't get into too much trouble if I went to college where our preacher went to school. For my parents, the first four reasons were trumped by the fifth … that Earl attended school there.

Recently, my Mama and my wife were chatting about me and Mama told her that I was sometimes a "handful" in my younger days. My wife would say I still am. They have a valid argument, I suppose.

Furman proved a good choice for all five of the above reasons.

Oh yeah, Earl … he was a cool guy. He could really take a joke. He preached a couple of sermons a week, read and studied a lot, went to a bunch of meetings, played a lot of golf, did weddings, funerals, visited sick and old folks.

From what I could tell, I believed the same things he believed. Both of us loved the Lord.

Earl was happy.

Hmmm, I made a note of Earl for future reference. What did he do?

Easy … Earl was a preacher.

Well, there were two things I thought I could do when I finished college.

Most importantly to me, both Fred and Earl seemed to be genuinely happy.

So, after my first year of college it was much easier to answer the question everybody was always asking.

What do you want to do?

I want to do what is required to become a salesman or a preacher.

The folks at church were excited about the preacher part.

I soon learned that becoming a preacher had conditions. First, you had to "feel called" to preach. It's a spiritual feeling to feel called to preach. I've never felt it. I tried to feel it. The harder I tried to feel called, the more I learned that trying to feel called is not exactly how it works. And the old devil loves young dumb-asses like me who were trying to feel called. It was clear by my actions that I wasn't being called.

My convictions hadn't changed. I just never felt the call. Preaching wasn't going to be an option.

I changed my "What do you want to do?" answer.

I want to become a salesman.

When I finished school in 1974, I learned a new word … recession. Who cared about what I wanted to do, I just wanted a job. I took a job in a big bank collecting money just to find out what I never wanted to do again.

When I got a call requesting that I interview for an internal sales position with a wholesale business across town, I jumped at the chance. I got the job. During my first few weeks at my new job, I saw a dozen or so professional salespeople in action and to my surprise, none of them seemed very happy.

Then … I met Luther.

Luther Hendrick was always singing, whistling, always had a skip in his step and a twinkle in his eye. If he liked you, he'd nickname you. He nicknamed me "Fluff." Well, it's hard to explain, but it had something to do with the extra skin on the side of my face that he thought made me look like I had a fluffy jaw. Luther reminded me of Fred. Luther didn't know it, but he had a new admirer. Luther's son Stan was to become a friend of mine, just like Fred's son.

Luther was happy.

Hmmm, there was no need to make any notes for future reference.

Luther became my happiness mentor. We went fishing twice a year in Panama City, Florida from 1976 until he retired in 1985. We played golf together every chance we got. Either one of us would drive a hundred miles out of the way just to play eighteen holes together. I remember hitting a terrible shot from the tee on a par three one day that rolled over a hundred yards before it went into the hole for my first hole-in-one. Luther cussed me like a dog for being so lucky but he was the first to walk into the clubhouse and tell the pro about my accomplishment. The cub pro exclaimed, "Congratulations son. You've just won a new Corvette!" I nearly fainted. Well, there was no Corvette, but I did win a free round of golf and Luther made sure my hole-in-one was registered with the USGA and my name listed on the club plaque.

We went deer hunting, quail and grouse hunting, fishing, and he even let me help him set up a dove shoot or two on his farm in Bowman. We stomped all over Georgia doing just about everything except work. When we did work, we always closed the sale. Yes, Luther was definitely my happiness mentor. Luther wasn't too much of anything else for me, he just went about being happy and he made me happy. I loved every minute I ever spent with him. I loved him. Whenever I was around Luther, he made me smile. Perfect.

And at last, I was doing what I wanted to do. I was a salesman.

Unlike Greer, I changed industries a couple of times before I settled into an area in which I was able to excel. I was self-employed the majority of my career. Even though I was signing the checks, I never stopped selling. I loved what I did. I was always happy throughout my career. I loved to go to work every day.

Luther died of cancer in 1990. He was only sixty-eight.

Lord, he was so much fun.

After he died, his son Stan gave me Luther's briefcase. He said that his dad wanted me to have it. The briefcase contains a W. D. Alexander Company product specification notebook, the last order pad he ever used, a stack of his business cards wrapped in a rubber band, and a half empty bottle of Mylanta. I keep Luther's briefcase in my office today.

He was the most colorful and fun person I've ever known. He was an original.

Luther was happy.

I saw Fred at a funeral recently.

Fred is eighty-five. He was sitting on the other side of the chapel. When I approached him, I didn't know if he would recognize me so I was prepared to re-introduce myself. As I extended my hand to shake his, his face broke into a big grin as he loudly exclaimed, "Well, hello there 'Davy Crockett'! Where's old 'Casper'?"

Some things never change. Fred was humming a song as he walked away to his car. Still a song in his heart, he is as happy as ever.

Fred ... is a happy man.

Fred and Luther, thank God both of you were a part of my life. I know why y'all were always happy ... it was simply because you decided to be. It really doesn't matter what you do ... whether you are a doctor or a ditch digger, if you decide to be happy ... you will be.

Forty years later, I did what I wanted to do and I am what I wanted to be.

Happy.

To All the Oysters I've Loved Before

"He was a bold man that first eat an oyster."
~ Jonathan Swift (1667-1745)

I ate my first raw oyster in the spring of 1976.

In 1976, at the tender age of twenty-four, I had become a proverbial traveling salesman. I traveled across the blacktop two-lane roads of South Georgia seeing small businesses in small towns. While traveling near St. Mary's in April of that year, I remembered that Joe had moved back home from Atlanta to open an insurance agency. I called Joe to say hello and he invited me over to his dad's place on the river for a seafood supper after work. I loved fresh fried seafood. I didn't realize that seafood was ever cooked any other way and I wasn't going to pass up the opportunity to enjoy it with a friend's family. Joe Harrison's dad, "Big Joe," was a newspaper publisher in St. Mary's, Georgia, and he lived on the Crooked (pronounced "Crook-id") River just outside of town. I couldn't wait to get there.

What I didn't bargain for in the process was the encounter with my first raw oyster.

While standing on the dock behind Mr. Harrison's house, he asked me if I liked oysters. My response was an enthusiastic "Yes, Sir" (again, unaware that they were prepared any way other than fried) and he proceeded to go to the refrigerator on the dock, open it, and take out a gallon of freshly shucked raw oysters. To my horror he poured more than a cup full of the slimy things into a drinking glass and topped it off with some of his homemade cocktail sauce. He smiled at me as he handed me the glass and said, "I shucked these myself." There must have been a couple dozen of the cold slime balls looking up at me from that glass.

Over the next thirty minutes, before we sat down to dinner, I did everything I could to choke down that glass full of oysters ... this including pouring the last six or eight oysters into the aforementioned Crooked River. I felt pretty "crook-id" myself after his smiling "I shucked these myself" comment. Over the rail of the dock, into the rising tide, gone. Thank God that was over.

After the glass full of oysters had been emptied, we were called to dinner. A wonderful home cooked fried seafood meal awaited. At the table that night I silently vowed to myself never to eat another cold, slimy raw oyster again.

Two weeks later, I never craved anything more in my life.

My lifelong addiction to raw oysters had begun.

There has never been a better time to eat them than in October. Ah, the chill in the night air begins to bring the changes of autumn to the South. Rich in tradition, the high school, college, and professional football seasons are in their full glory. Locally grown apples in the North Georgia Mountains around the town of Ellijay will be harvested. The leaves of the hardwood forests will begin to turn colors. Most wonderfully, the chill in the air means the oysters of the Gulf will begin to become colder, saltier, and thus, "in season."

Time to eat.

My annual October pilgrimage in search of the glorious mollusks begins anytime after my birthday, October 13th. It always ends with the same destination ... Hunt's Oyster Bar, Panama City, Florida.

After my initial encounter in 1976 with the raw oysters on "Big Joe's" dock in St. Mary's, I was drawn by the legend of how perfect the oysters from the Apalachicola River were in the fall of the year. They are harvested in Apalachicola Bay where the fresh water river flows into the salt waters of the Gulf of Mexico. The tasty morsels are their salty best as the temperatures begin to drop in October through the winter.

I tasted my first oyster at Hunt's Oyster Bar in October 1977. I haven't missed an October trip since then (well, except for the time that Hunt's burned and they had to rebuild it and didn't re-open until November that year). All of Hunt's oysters are from the Apalachicola River.

After a day's ride from my home in Atlanta, I arrive late in the afternoon just before the local crowd gets off work and begins pouring into the restaurant to get their daily fix. With a tall glass of sweet tea in hand, I belly up to the bar where I will stay and eat oysters until I've had my fill. The skilled oyster "shuckers" keep my tray filled as I stuff myself. Freshly shucked oysters right out of the shell with Hunt's special sauce ... divine.

An old oyster shucker at Hunt's shared a secret with me about the art of eating raw oysters thirty years ago. He looked at me through his leathery eyelids and simply said, "Son, don't ever eat an oyster on a cracker." It proved to be one of the great culinary lessons of my life. In order to keep up with the local shuckers that work at Hunt's, I simply savor oysters in the sauce with one quick bite and they're gone. The one and only time I tried to eat crackers with them, the crackers went down at an angle and took up too much room where the oysters could've gone. No saltine cracker would ever again occupy the space reserved for an oyster. I vowed to follow the tough old oyster shucker's advice. Never again has there been an oyster on a cracker on my plate. I have kept that vow and taught all of my children to do the same.

God bless my mother for giving birth to me in October.

My favorite gift each year awaits in a little oyster bar in Panama City.

One Golf Swing and Other Important Stuff

I have had over thirty years to reflect on the one golf lesson Davis Love, Jr. gave me on that Tuesday morning in 1979.

It wasn't just a golf lesson ... it was a lesson on patience, leadership, and life.

My wife and I had moved to St. Simons Island, Georgia, from Atlanta in 1977 with the company I represented as a salesman. My responsibilities included traveling throughout the southern portion of Georgia. I was twenty-five years old.

The same year, Davis Love, Jr. left his position as the head golf professional at the Atlanta Country Club and along with his wife, Penta, and two sons, Davis III and Mark, moved to St. Simons Island to become the head teaching professional at Sea Island Golf Club. Mr. Love was forty-two years old.

My training for the sales position I had taken with my company was elementary. They gave me a catalog of our products, particular sales programs, a price sheet, an existing customer list, and an order pad with carbon paper. "Go sell something" was my charge. Those were the days ... I was a green kid with no business acumen other than a deep conviction that "The Golden Rule" would be my guide. I had big aspirations and not a clue about how to start. What I lacked in experience I would counter with effort.

In Texas during the 1950s, Mr. Love was a student of the legendary golf coach Harvey Penick. Penick was the master of a simple, commonsense approach to the game. Davis Love, Jr. had excelled at his craft by winning numerous PGA tournaments. He competed and led in tournaments that included iconic names such as Palmer, Hogan, Nicklaus, Snead, and Player in the field of players. Perhaps most importantly, he had shown the unique ability to teach the same level of skills he was able to execute on his own. He had carved his niche as a world-class teaching pro and was arriving at Sea Island Golf Club on Georgia's coast to ply his trade on the legendary links course.

Growing up in Atlanta during my childhood, Davis Love, Jr. was larger than life because of the reputation that he had attained as a professional golfer, both on the PGA Tour and as a local course's "Head Pro."

He was a professional.

I was a bogey golfer. I rarely broke ninety. I could only fantasize that someday I could shoot a par round of seventy-two.

A couple years passed and as fate would have it, both of our families became members of First Baptist Church of St. Simons Island. I had taken the responsibility of teaching a teenaged young men's Sunday school class. In the class were Mr. and Mrs. Love's boys, Davis III and Mark.

It was unusual to see Mr. Love in church on Sunday morning because of the conflict of timing with his responsibilities of teaching on the weekends at the golf club. One Sunday he was there. When church was over, the congregation always became congested as we exited the front door where Dr. Felix Haynes, our pastor, always waited with an outstretched hand and an eager smile. I was making my way to the door and I happened to be standing by the Love family. I simply spoke to Mr. Love and explained that a friend and I were Davis and Mark's Sunday school class teachers. He was gracious in his response. After two years, I finally worked up the guts to have broken the ice for my first conversation with one of the legendary local sports figures of my childhood.

I have no idea why I said it ... I suppose I figured it's now or never Dave, so standing right in the aisle at the church I just blurted out, "Ya' know, Mr. Love, I'm trying my best to keep both of your boys out of Hell teaching them about the Lord in Sunday school and well, I don't have the first idea of how to straighten out my fade and I couldn't draw the ball if my life depended on it." Whew, I did it. I asked for his help.

Thankfully, when Mr. Love stopped chuckling, he said, "I think I could probably help you with your fade and your draw. Could you come by the club Tuesday and have lunch with me?" I gave him a nervous one word response ... "Absolutely!"

I took the day off Tuesday.

I got to the golf club a little before noon and as promised, Mr. Love was expecting me. He asked where I had parked and after telling him I had parked by the practice range he asked me to go and get my seven-iron and meet him at the practice tee while he went to get some balls for me to hit. I was waiting at the practice tee when I saw him coming across the parking lot with a little green bag that might have contained six or seven range balls. As he approached, all I could think was that I had never made a golf ball draw in my life; surely, it was going to take more shots than the amount of balls he was bringing with him to help me.

I was wrong.

He dropped the first golf ball at my feet and asked me to address the ball and hit it with my normal swing. I did and predictably, the ball started slightly to the left and faded back to the right about 165 yards away. He simply said, "Mmm hmm, very good." He dropped the second golf ball at my feet and then added, "Take your normal stance and this time move your left hand to the right until you can see three knuckles, then simply cover your left thumb with your right hand." By doing as he had instructed, I had changed my grip by moving both hands about an inch to my right. Then he asked me to hit it with my normal swing. I did and a miracle happened ... on one swing. I hit a perfect draw about 165 yards. Mr. Love looked up at me, smiled a knowing smile of satisfaction, and said, "That was easy. Let's have lunch!"

He had corrected the flaw in my swing with just one ball. Amazing. Was I standing on "Holy Ground"?

That afternoon, delivered with unspoken elegance, Davis Love Jr. gave me a simple and invaluable lesson that has had a lasting impact. Simple solutions have always yielded the most effective results. Countless times over the next three decades I have followed his instructions. I have never forgotten what he taught me.

He first asked me to demonstrate my skills.

Having observed the results, he analyzed the issues with the execution of my swing.

Then, using the common sense approach of his mentor, he participated in the correction of the issues by suggesting a simple behavior modification, *i.e.,* I moved both hands to the right about an inch.

Finally, he evaluated my second shot and verified that I understood his analysis by correctly executing the shot as he had instructed.

A successful golf shot was the result.

Unconsciously, I noted his process. Be patient with his process. Trust his process. Always use his process.

First, Demonstrate.

Second, Observe.

Third, Participate.

Fourth, Evaluate.

Repeat as necessary until the desired results are attained. When the results are attained, move to the next opportunity. Common sense. Simple solutions. Sound methods.

Over a lunch of shrimp salad sandwiches he asked me about myself, my profession, my family, my plans and such, then before I left that day he asked me to wait and said he had something for me. He shook my hand, chuckling as he thanked me for having his kids in our Sunday school class and for my part in keeping his boys out of Hell.

As I was leaving the golf club he handed me a gift, a brand new "Acushnet Bulls Eye" putter. When he handed it to me he quietly said, "Trust your swing, Dave. Just keep playing and you will shoot par one day."

After that Tuesday, I saw him only in passing, yet I always admired him.

A few years later, my career took me away from St. Simons Island, but nothing could ever take St. Simons Island and our innocent years there away from me.

Mr. Love died tragically in a plane crash in November of 1988. I, along with the entire golfing community, still grieve his family's and the world of golf's loss.

On a bright Wednesday afternoon in the autumn of 1990, at Whitepath Golf Course near Ellijay in the mountains of north Georgia ... I shot par seventy-two.

Sterile as a Stainless Steel Operating Table

In the winter of 1985, we were the proud parents of two boys—Greg, six and Andy, two.

After varied discussions and a satisfactory time to think about our decision, we decided that our family was complete. Beverly had been taking birth control pills for over ten years to help with our family planning. We both agreed that it would be a prudent decision for us to consider other family planning options for her health.

The summary of our options concluded that I should have a vasectomy. Fun ... how did I ever let myself get into the position to have volunteered to do that? Somebody call me a "shrink"!

We lived in a small South Georgia town in a nice home out in the country at the end of a dirt road. There weren't any vasectomy doctors for miles. The only people who could've helped me in this town were veterinarians, and they were more accustomed to making eunuchs out of their four-legged patients.

I was definitely leaving town for this procedure.

On D-Day for the family jewels, an older neighbor, Liz, came over to stay with Greg and Andy while we drove to Brunswick to go through with my ordeal. Living in a small town meant that Liz and everybody else in the county knew that I was going to have a vasectomy that morning in Brunswick. Trying to help, she confided that her husband, Jim, had the same thing done and there was nothing to it. I smiled and acted sincere when she made this attempt of compassion for my impending doom. The only thing I could think when she was talking was that I should be talking to Jim about this, not Liz.

Upon arrival at the doctor's office where the procedure was to take place, I was instructed to remove my trousers for "prep." Nobody told me about prep. Prep involved a razor and shaving cream and I did not have control of the razor. I was already nervous and someone standing over me with a razor did not help my anxiety. After being prepped and numbed with a local anesthetic in all the right places (enough said), my doctor Jack and his surgical nurse Jill arrived.

Jack and Jill? Really?

Dear Lord ... I should have known better than to be doing this.

We arrived home later that night without any fanfare. I thought to myself, "Liz was right. There is nothing to it." Of course, I was still numb. When I awoke in the middle of the night the local anesthetic had worn off and I could feel some discomfort but nothing to be too alarmed about. It was only when I stood to walk to the bathroom that I was surprised by the unfamiliar weight below my belt. Okay, maybe Liz was wrong. My testicles felt like they weighted twenty pounds each. Carefully supporting them with my hand, I shuffled to the bathroom. This was going to be a longer recovery than I had expected.

Six weeks later, I drove myself back to see Dr. Jack and Jill for my post-operative checkup. After a particularly unmentionable test was successfully completed, Dr. Jack and Jill assured me that I was walking out of that office as "sterile as a stainless steel operating table."

I recovered from the trauma and our lives went back to normal. A little over a year later, my wife developed what we thought was a stomach bug. However, her upset stomach became a chronic condition. She was losing weight, her complexion paled and she even had to cancel a piano concert she was scheduled to play. Canceling a concert was serious business and something she would have never considered if she weren't really sick. We were worried and decided she needed to see the doctor for her condition.

The local doctors tried to help but couldn't find any cause for her illness. Our local doctor decided she needed to see specialists and sent her to thoracic and gastroenterology specialists in Brunswick and Jacksonville.

After tests and more tests that took more than a month to complete, a scan showed a mass in her abdomen. We feared the worst. More blood tests were ordered and we returned home to nervously await the results.

The doctor's office called, explaining that there were no indications of disease from the test results and that in fact we should be pleased with the results. We were. All of the blood tests came back negative except for one ... the pregnancy test.

Yep ... the pregnancy test.

When the nurse announced that the pregnancy test was positive, Beverly explained that she couldn't be pregnant because her husband was a proud member of the fraternity of caring noble men that had endured the knife during the awful and humbling experience of a vasectomy. Okay, okay ... she probably didn't say it exactly like that, but she was quite insistent that she could not be pregnant because her husband had undergone a vasectomy over a year ago.

On the other end, the nurse (probably rolling her eyes and yawning) said simply, "Honey, if you're Beverly Brown and you live at Route Seven, Baxley, Georgia ... you're pregnant."

The mass in her abdomen had arms and legs!

After her initial shock and tears, we became excited that our family was about to expand.

After a visit to her obstetrician in Brunswick for a routine sonogram, we left the doctor's office with the first pictures of our baby. I had a particularly clear one tucked in my pocket.

I had a special stop to make with that picture. I wanted to show some special friends of mine ... remember Jack and Jill?

I can't verbalize the kick I got out of handing them the sonogram and explaining that I wasn't as "sterile as a stainless steel operating table." The look on their faces, mouths hanging wide open, hands hanging limp at their sides ... well, some things just can't be put into words. Jack was stunned and offered his apologies. I just smiled and explained that the good Lord knows more than we do about what we need and we must need another baby. I was thrilled.

Seven months later, on December 8, 1986, Ashley Susannah Brown was born.

She is and will always be her Daddy's little girl ... and if you just have to know ... she looks just like me.

Thank heaven for little girls!

The "Spumoni" of My Life

I love ice cream. I like all kinds of flavors, although my favorite flavor is vanilla. Vanilla ice cream goes with everything and can be mixed with anything. I think that's why it's my favorite.

Our family had pretty ordinary tastes in ice cream.

Beverly couldn't get enough chocolate, Greg preferred vanilla, and strawberry was Andy's favorite. Andy would reach for the freezer when he was a toddler begging for straw"betty" ice cream! A half-gallon of Neapolitan ice cream served as an ideal dessert at the end of most meals.

And then, out of nowhere, we were introduced to an incomparably complex flavor ... spumoni. We all loved it.

The addition of "spumoni" in our house changed all of our lives.

My baby girl Ashley was born on a Monday. She would have been a surprise to most, a real surprise. A couple of years after my successful vasectomy kind of surprise!

I believe that she was our family's little spumoni miracle!

I couldn't have been more pleased when we visited the doctor for a routine sonogram and were told that our baby was a girl.

The boys would have a baby sister. Beverly would have a daughter.

I would have a Daddy's little girl! We would name her Ashley.

Ashley was to be delivered by Caesarian section on a Wednesday, a planned delivery by the same doctor who had delivered our two sons.

Ashley was enthusiastic even before she was born and decided she would come into this world when she was good and ready.

And she was ready . . . two days early. Early for Ashley was to become her "on time."

That was just the beginning of the spell that she cast on me.

I have always been a punctual person. I learned about being on time from my Dad, who was notoriously punctual. Born two days ahead of schedule, Ashley entered the world as punctual as her "PaPa," my Dad. Eventually, she would verbalize her philosophy regarding punctuality. It went like this (she grinned the entire time she explained): "Early is on time Daddy, on time is late . . . Daddy, let's be early, PWEEEEEEEEASE be early, okay?"

Pink. She loved pink. I bought her everything I could find in pink. Pink ribbons. Pink socks. Pink dresses. Pink pajamas. Pink bows. Pink jeans. Pink shirts. Pink underwear. Pink hats. Pink pillows. Forgive me PETA, I even found her a shaggy little pink fur coat.

My favorite pink "thing" wasn't a thing at all. They were "things," a pair of pink "Jellies." Jellies were little colored plastic sandals popular in the late 1980s and early 1990s. Even as young as three, she would call me at work just to talk. She called me one day at work and asked me if I would go by Wal-Mart and bring her a pair of Jellies. She was very specific about the color she wanted. "Pink, NOT 'Geeen' (green) Daddy, Pink . . . I NEEEEEEEED them."

She wore her pink Jellies everywhere. They were her favorite shoes. Naturally, on our vacation to Washington, D.C. she wore her beloved pink Jellies. While crossing the street from the National Mall to one of the Smithsonian Museums, the Jelly on her tiny right foot slipped off and was left in the street. Scooping her up into my arms as we hurried through the crosswalk she shrieked into my ear, "Daddy, my Jelly!" She was pointing to her shoe lying in the middle of the road. Just as we turned to look, we watched a twelve-ton city bus drive over the top of the little pink Jelly.

When the bus passed, her favorite little Jelly lay squished as flat as a piece of paper in the middle of the road.

The realization of her loss was immediate. She burst into tears as all of us just stared at the flattened little plastic shoe.

And then… the tiny pink sandal proved to be incredibly resilient.

Her little pink Jelly began to regain its original shape. Slowly but surely, the improbable became real. We stepped back into the crosswalk where the little shoe rested and just like in *Cinderella* the shoe fit her tiny foot like a glove.

She wore them every day until she just couldn't squeeze her growing feet into them anymore.

Today, the little pair of five inch long pink Jellies rest on display in the china cabinet in our home and are one of my most prized possessions. Who knows, with their proven resilience they may just last forever. They will last forever in my heart.

Ruffles. Could a little girl have too many ruffles?

Contrary to the stereotypical American male, I love shopping with any of the women in my life. It's a trait that I learned from my mother. Mama has a doctorate degree in shopping.

Ashley and I went shopping together for an Easter dress on a spring Saturday. Just the two of us, for her we might as well have been in Paris during Fashion Week. She knew exactly what she wanted and we would shop until we found it. I hoped that it might involve ruffles.

It proved to be a long day. Hours of shopping and we still hadn't found what she wanted, but we weren't going home without it. Forward we trekked from town to town, store to store, rack to rack in search of the perfect Easter dress.

And suddenly, it appeared.

A perfect little white dress with black polka dots the size of half dollars all over it. It was a long-waist pattern with a black sash that surrounded her little hips and a bright red rose attached on the left hip.

And below the sash . . . ruffles! Lots of them!

She saw it and gasped. "Daddy, can I please have that one? I NEEEEEEEED it!"

It was a perfect fit. I have never seen anything prettier than Ashley in that little white dress. Over twenty years later, I can still picture her in that dress and the memory still warms my heart.

Curls. How can you not love a little girl's curls?

Our home rested on property bordering a national forest in the North Georgia Mountains. Nature and all its glory at our back door, it wasn't unusual for wildlife to be spotted in our yard. Fox, chipmunks, opossum, deer, turtles, rabbits, bobcats, raccoons, skunks, hawks, squirrels, and even an occasional bear were always close by.

With no close neighbors, her only playmates were her two older brothers. She insisted that they play "weddings" and dolls together and they made sure that she could catch anything that crawls. They were constant companions. Playing outside with her two brothers involved countless memorable adventures of every kind. I loved the way her hair would curl when exposed to the legendary humidity of our Southern summer days. The longer she stayed outside, the curlier her hair became.

On a particular Sunday afternoon in April, my little precious innocent Ashley made an exciting new discovery and came running to share it with me.

As she burst into the room breathless with excitement it was clear to me that she had just seen something amazing. She had just made a new discovery in the blue sky above our yard. With curls bouncing, face flushed red, and little chest heaving, she exclaimed, "Daddy, Daddy, I've just seen 'a few of eagles' . . . and they were all crying, 'CAW, CAW, CAW'!" She'd spied a flock of crows. I've never see a crow without thinking of my beautiful daughter and her excitement over "a few of eagles" on that spring day.

Always early! A pair of little pink Jellies, a polka dot Easter dress with a red rose and ruffles, and "a few of eagles."

Yep, I sure do like ice cream. I like chocolate, vanilla and strawberry… but, I LOVE SPUMONI!

Mickey Mantle, My Boys and Me

"Show me a hero and I will write you a tragedy."
~ F. Scott Fitzgerald

Turning his nine-iron upside down and using it like a cane, he slowly ambled up the incline of the elevated tee. He was on the seventeenth hole of Harbor Club's lakeside course in Lake Oconee, Georgia. Having been kicked in the shin during a football game as a youth, he had developed Osteomyelitis in his leg (an infection of the bone and the bone marrow). His leg was saved from amputation by the use of a relatively new drug called penicillin; the injury plagued him throughout the rest of his life. It was a Saturday afternoon in April of 1991. At fifty-nine, both legs were bowed like the cowboys who roamed his native Oklahoma just a generation before he was born. His name was synonymous with the childhood of any American boy that had ever held a bat and ball and grew up in the 1950s.

Mickey Mantle.

As was the case with innumerable boys of the 1950s, he was my childhood.

Listening to the radio on a Friday in April, I learned that Mickey Mantle was hosting a Make-A-Wish Foundation golf event at Harbor Club on Lake Oconee the following day. He had purchased a lakefront condominium there several years earlier and had come to consider the small rural town his second home. I was thirty-eight years old and had two sons—Greg, twelve and Andy, eight.

My boys and I loaded into my pickup truck the following morning and made the drive in search of the golf course on Lake Oconee just for the chance to see "The Mick."

Upon our arrival, we learned that Mickey would be on the seventeenth tee all day challenging the Make-A-Wish tournament participants and their celebrity hosts to a "closest to the pin" contest on the course's signature par three to raise money for the charity. Each player anted up twenty-five dollars for the shot and then Mickey hit his ball first. If the players got closer to the pin than Mantle he would personally autograph a baseball for them. If not, the consolation was a picture of you and your foursome made with Mickey standing in front of a sponsor's new car.

Our course was set. We would watch from behind the tee with the hope of just catching a glimpse of the great New York Yankee Hall of Fame slugger. Our day would be complete. We got in place behind the tee and were lucky enough to get a nice plot of grass directly beside the rope barrier that would serve to control the crowd. We were going to be close to all of the fun!

The name of the hole that was to be Mickey's stage that Saturday was "The Marsh". "The Marsh" was, itself, considered to be one of Georgia's eighteen most challenging holes. The hole required a shot of 180 yards that was completely over water to a small green. The cup was in the far back left of the green. The tee was slightly elevated and was approximately thirty yards deep. Mickey would challenge all of the participants from the tee that was 159 yards to the pin. For most of the amateur golfers that meant the club selection would be a seven-iron. Not for Mickey, who once confessed that he tried to hit a home run every time he swung the bat. For him that meant the club of choice would be a nine-iron and that he would swing it as hard as possible. A low line drive draw that consistently curled up close to the pin was usually the result.

Mickey arrived via golf cart and riding with him was Hank Bauer, his first New York Yankee roommate.

Upon arriving at the tee they were each gracious to the crowd, waving and wishing all a good time. They were clearly having fun and we could hear them talking about "old times" with the Yankee teams of the 1950s. They were just kids back in the early 1950s themselves and were acting like they still might have a childish bone or two in their bodies. Soon we would see that they did. We were only fifty feet away from them. My boys and I were thrilled to be so close.

Lexus had just introduced their initial flagship model, the LS400, and the company was sponsoring the seventeenth hole that day by offering a new car to any player that made a hole-in-one on the shot competing with Mickey. Additionally, Lexus placed one of the cars on the rear of the tee box so the players could be photographed with Mickey in front of it as a keepsake of their involvement in the tournament.

Hank and Mickey arrived with mischief on their minds and they had a plan to see that they caused plenty.

Hank brought a thick black rubber snake and a large fishing pole with him to the tee. The artificial snake was attached to the fishing pole with a strong line and then hidden in the bushes on the far side of the seventeenth tee box. Hank hid in the bushes on the near side of the tee box. Before the players and celebrities hit the competitive shots with Mickey they would pose for a picture with him in front of the shiny new car. When the players stood to be photographed with Mickey, Hank would begin reeling the big black rubber snake in front of them and Mickey, pointing down, would scream, "SNAKE"! All of the players would run different directions, some shrieking as they ran. Former Baltimore Colt NFL football great Tom Matte actually jumped up on the trunk of the new Lexus with metal cleats and, well, made quite an impression. This literally caused Mantle to fall down laughing, over and over again. All of the fun was for the pleasure of the crowd and participants alike.

After Matte's encounter, Mickey had to tell every player exactly how it had happened. He laughed harder telling them the story than when it actually happened. It just got funnier and funnier to remember Matte dancing a jig with metal cleats on the Lexus. This went on for hours as the foursomes of players and their celebrity played through.

Dozens of Major League Baseball Hall of Fame athletes played through; Yogi Berra, "Whitey" Ford, Lew Burdette, Harmon Killebrew, Warren Spahn, and NFL legend Johnny Unitas, just to name a few. Then, as the day was getting close to an end, there was a brief gap in the action at the seventeenth tee because the next foursome of players had as their celebrity PGA Hall of Fame golfer Tom Weiskopf. Tom was the course designer and his group was taking their time playing the course. This simply meant that there was about fifteen minutes until their group arrived to challenge Mickey as they were about a hole behind all of the other foursomes.

There was a short pause and then it happened.

Mickey took his nine-iron and turned it upside down and leaning down on it, began walking toward the crowd. People were trying to woo him closer to seek his autograph. He seemed oblivious as if he were headed to a specific predetermined destination. As he continued his deliberate stroll down the tee, I said to the boys, "Look guys, he is so close."

Ten seconds later, he was there.

Using his nine-iron for support, he crouched down onto one knee right in front of my boys and me. He looked into Andy's eyes, extended his right hand and said, "Hi Buddy, I'm Mickey Mantle". Andy reached up, placed his left hand in Mickey's right hand and responded, "I'm Andy." Mickey smiled and asked Andy who the fellow next to him was. Andy said that it was his big brother, Greg. Mickey smiled, offered Greg his right hand and said, "Hi Greg, I hope you're having fun." Greg extended his right hand into Mickey's and exclaimed, "Hi ya' Mick!" Mickey smiled his genuine, larger-than-life "aw shucks" smile at Greg and turned to me.

He put his arm around my shoulder, pulled me close to him and said, "I've been watching you all day with your boys. I want you to know that

I'd give anything I have to be able to spend one more day with my boys, just sitting in the grass enjoying one another like I've watched you do today. I'd trade places with you if I could."

As he rose and turned away to begin his climb back up to the tee, I knew I would never be the same. The hero of my youth, a legend, had just reached out and for a moment wished we could have changed places. I understood.

Just over four years later, on August 13, 1995, I sat in the floor of our den with my boys and we cried together when the word came on the television that Mickey Mantle had died of liver cancer. My mind raced back to that perfect day in April when he wrapped his arm around me.

Today, I'm almost fifty-nine and I remember the wise words that Mickey Mantle humbly and sincerely offered to me when he was exactly my age. I always think of his wish whenever I am together with my boys. Greg is thirty-two and lives in Oregon and Andy is twenty-eight and lives in Texas. Still, with distances and years separating us from that moment with Mickey, the three of us remember everything about that day ... the sound of Mickey's laughter, even the smell of the grass. None of us will ever forget that pure and innocent moment together.

You can never diminish the importance of a positive role model. The world is full of them. You just have to be aware.

Flawed though he was, Mickey Mantle was a hero to millions of kids. More importantly, he was a hero to me.

Mickey was once quoted as saying, "All I ever had was natural ability." Well, with his debilitating injuries ... the effort it took for him to successfully execute his "natural ability" into a professional Hall of Fame career was nothing short of herculean. It was heroic.

I've had my fair share of medical issues over the past twenty years. The way he overcame his physical adversity makes me strive to work harder to overcome mine. And overcome them, I have.

And while Mickey's insightful words that he said to me on that April day make me long to be a better role model ... I think now, more than ever, we need people who are not afraid to try and hit a home run every time they come to bat.

What we really need are more heroes.

"Do Yourself a Favor, Take a Kid Fishing"

Before any of my children were born, in the mid-1970s, I enjoyed watching a Saturday night fishing show called *The Southern Sportsman*. The host of the show, Franc White, was an outdoorsman, hunter, fisherman, commentator, writer, restaurateur, environmentalist (he was ahead of his time), and chef from North Carolina. Every week we watched him fish in one of his favorite fishing holes and then cook what he caught as part of the show's entertainment. Franc, still alive and fishing at eighty-five, currently lives an active life in North Carolina.

Franc ended every show the same way. He always said, "Do yourself a favor, take a kid fishing."

I recall so many of the fishing trips that my boys, Greg and Andy, and I took with each other. Just being together was always fun for us. Although most of our days were spent without so much as a nibble . . . there were quite a few memorable exceptions.

Amongst endless rows of neatly planted pine trees, at a buddy, "Chubby" Teston's pond on Penholloway Road, near the Altamaha River, little four-year-old Andy's Zebco Model 33 reel sung like a squealing piglet as he fought the fish on the end of his line. When the rod finally went limp he had caught a five-pound channel catfish nearly as long as he was. I've never seen a bigger smile than the one on his older brother's face as he proclaimed, "I've always wanted a little brother just like you." Greg was eight and as far as he was concerned, Andy catching his first fish was a historic event. He was right.

It was the first fish he'd ever caught and it was a monster.

Greg developed an interest in fly-fishing. He practiced his casts in the yard for days upon end, waiting for the time to come to fish a mountain river. When that day finally came it was like a scene from Norman Maclean's *A River Runs Through It*. Amidst towering hemlock trees entwined with giant white pines, a pristine stream descended down the mountain. Greg was fishing upstream from the base of a series of small waterfalls and ripples, placing the lures as naturally as possible above where the trout would be waiting, letting the bait float down the creek, tempting the trout below the surface. Suddenly there was a shout downstream, "Daddy, I got one!" Greg came running with his first trout in one hand, his fly rod in the other, along through the mountain laurel and rhododendron lined path that covered the banks of Noontootla Creek near where it crossed the Appalachian Trail. He was breathless having caught his first trout on a fly rod, the reward of countless hours of practice casting in preparation for this single moment. He was thirteen.

A few years later, while fishing on a friend's property that bordered Tickanetley Creek, Andy was casting into a deep, shady hole underneath the purple blooms of a huge old rhododendron that hung heavily over the rippling waters of the stream when the old rainbow trout struck his lure. After a fight with the big fish, he landed it in his net. Andy ran several hundred feet straight up the middle of the creek, holding his fish over his head, exclaiming his accomplishment for all that had ears to hear. He frightened every fish, snake, bird, cat, dog, cow, bear or any other creature within a mile, to death. It was to be the only fish that would be caught from that part of the creek that day. My old friend Dwayne still laughs about Andy's sprint up the creek with his fish in his hand. Dwayne says he can still hear Andy's voice echoing from the precious memories.

It was the first trout that he ever caught. Believe me, Andy was more surprised than the trout. Andy was twelve.

On the road where we lived near Athens was a little lake called Betty Garrett's Pond. Betty was married to Dick and I still don't know why it was only Betty's pond but I never heard it referred to any other way. Might've been because Betty was the warden of the pond ... the neighborhood kids could only fish when she wanted them to fish and her word was law.

In Betty Garrett's Pond resided a largemouth bass the neighborhood kids named "The Ghost." The Ghost lived in the deepest parts of the pond and only on the rarest occasions would he silently lurk in the shadows of the reeds and the nearby overhanging pine boughs, showing himself to the kids as though teasing them, furthering his legendary status amongst the neighborhood boys. As the sightings continued, the legend of the fish grew. Friends from their school knew of the elusive largemouth bass and considered it a local mystery. This was one seriously cool fish.

How large was it?

What did it eat?

How old was it?

Could it possibly be caught?

The Ghost was the coolest fish in the world to all of those kids.

Greg and Andy always kept a rod ready in case The Ghost suddenly appeared. Baited with a one-ounce Johnson Silver Spoon, the twenty-pound test line was affixed to a bait-casting reel on a six-foot long stiff rod.

I had never seen The Ghost.

On a cold winter Saturday afternoon, that changed.

The unmistakable shadow of the "lunker" appeared and Greg sent the Silver Spoon to within inches of the fish. The Ghost swiftly turned and struck the intruder of its underwater world and the fight was on. Some ten minutes later Greg had landed the legend! With The Ghost in hand, he ran the half-mile back to our house, screaming to the world that he had conquered his greatest adversary. Mt. Everest had been climbed! For Greg, Hemingway had never written about as great a fish. He had caught The Ghost!

Almost twenty years later, The Ghost now resides over the fireplace in Greg's home in the mountains near Jacksonville, Oregon. And, yes, the legendary bass is still the coolest fish in the world. Above the mantle, The Ghost is wearing sunglasses.

Some years later, our family scheduled a summer vacation for July that would lead us throughout the Florida Keys. The boys and I planned to do a little tarpon fishing while we were there.

On July 5th, while still anticipating our summer vacation, our world was rocked. I had a grand mal seizure and after being rushed to the hospital and undergoing surgery, I was diagnosed with an inoperable cancerous brain tumor. I was forty-three. My prognosis was grim and I began chemotherapy and radiation treatments that would continue through the next year.

Greg graduated from high school the following year and left home to pursue his own life's adventures. He simply said that he didn't want to go to college until he'd seen the great rivers of the West and fished them all. We didn't blame him. With our blessings, he began his journey that continues today.

In 1998, with Greg living and fishing in Montana, the rest of our family began the vacation that we had planned two years before that none of the doctors thought we would ever be able to take.

A few days later we arrived in Islamorada, a fishing town in the Florida Keys where Andy and I were planning to fish for tarpon.

The tarpon guide picked us up at three o'clock the following morning. As we helped gather bait and load the boat, Andy explained to our guide why this was an especially important trip for us. He told him of how Greg was to have come before and how he wished that he could have been with us today. The guide was very quietly empathetic, explaining that his dad had cancer as well.

After an hour's ride into the edges of the Everglades we arrived at our guide's favorite fishing hole. As the guide poled through "the flats," Andy followed his precise instructions where to cast his line baited with shrimp.

Silently we moved all around the area where the guide had taken us. Over an hour passed with no luck. Then it happened.

The sound broke the silence like a sudden slap from the palm of a giant's hand on the water. It was a most unnatural sound. We all jumped when we heard it. It was as though something huge had just sucked two or three gallons of water off of the surface at once with a huge and resounding GULP!

Our guide quietly turned to us and whispered, "Tarpon"!

In careful silence, he poled us around so that Andy could make the precise cast required.

When we reached the precise location our guide was seeking, he stepped silently to the front of the boat and up onto the casting deck and whispered to Andy, "Cast the bait as far as you can at about ten o'clock from my mark." Andy placed the bait perfectly in front of the tarpon and it immediately rose to the surface and struck the bait!

Andy set the hook and the fight was on.

Having been quiet for three hours, our excitement was uncontrolled and without reservation. As the fight progressed, our guide gleefully screamed instructions and encouragement to Andy, who executed the directions with flawless determination. We were all yelling with excitement at the sight of a seven-foot long fish "walking" across the water on its tail in hundred foot intervals! With the rising sun reflecting off its silver dollar sized scales, every imaginable color radiated from the tarpon's movements as it surfaced. While slinging its huge head from side to side as it came closer to our boat, the nearly 200-pound fish was drenching us with salt water. The wetter we became from salty rain being showered upon us, the more it seemed as though the magnificent creature with its mouth stretched fully open was simply having a grand laugh at each of us, just toying with us and our foolish efforts to tame its wild and wonderful life.

Andy released that trophy tarpon back into the waters of the Everglades. The three of us were exhausted. Sitting on the floor of the boat, we relived the grandness of our experience and smiled without speaking a word as each of us basked in the moment.

There wasn't a dry eye in the boat.

Catching a catfish in South Georgia, native trout in the clear waters near the Appalachian Trail, a legendary bass from a farm pond, and a trophy tarpon from the sparkling jewels of the Florida Keys ... each are burned into the film of our minds and will always share places in our hearts.

Of all the times my boys and I went fishing, I never actually remember catching a fish myself.

It was really all about being together.

"Cancer? ...
Did My Doctor Just Say Cancer?"

"... for the past two weeks you have been reading about a bad break I got. Yet today, ... I consider myself the luckiest man on the face of the earth."
~ Lou Gehrig

It was a normal morning on Friday, July 5, 1996.

I had worked the previous day collecting money from an out-of-town account in the North Georgia mountain town of Clayton. My family came with me that day and we made a holiday excursion out of an ordinary business trip. We really had a fun day together. When we got home, our neighbors Sue and LaVohn invited us over to their house to sit by the pool and celebrate the Fourth of July.

I was forty-three, my kids were seventeen, thirteen, and nine years old.

I awoke as usual the next day, used the bathroom, and returned to bed to snooze just a few more minutes before getting up to prepare to go to work.

My wife was still asleep at approximately seven o'clock that morning. She was startled awake by the sounds and movements of my uncontrollable thrashing in our bed. I was unconscious and was having what was later diagnosed as a grand mal seizure. The seizure lasted approximately fifteen minutes. Beverly called 911. She ran to get Greg, my oldest son, to care for me as the seizure continued. Greg used all of his considerable strength trying to keep me from hurting myself as I thrashed about in my unconscious condition. Bev and the other children awaited the ambulance outside. They wanted to make sure the emergency personnel found us in our rather rural location.

Terror seized them all.

The emergency medical team arrived as the seizure was ending and I was regaining consciousness. I awakened incredibly sore and disoriented. The EMTs checked my vital signs and strapped me onto a gurney for transport to Athens Regional Medical Center. I started to become lucid as the EMTs pushed the gurney into the ambulance. Greg climbed in behind me but the EMTs moved him to the front of the ambulance so they could treat me.

What was happening to me? Was I having a heart attack? No pain in my chest, no numbness in my arm, no shortness of breath and no feelings of nausea. That couldn't be it.

I heard the EMTs telling me that I had just had a seizure.

A what?

I was having a seizure? I was having a what? I'd heard of seizures and I was clueless as to why I would have had one. What makes you have a seizure? Maybe … epilepsy? How do you suddenly become epileptic? As my mind began to become clear it was filled with endless frantic questions.

Beverly, Andy, and Ashley followed closely behind the speeding ambulance the entire twenty-mile journey to the hospital, frantic for news about my condition. While en route, the emergency technicians monitored my vital signs and were in constant contact with the hospital on a speakerphone. At about the halfway point one of the emergency technicians shouted in a frantic voice, "We're losing him!"

Am I dreaming? Am I really dying?

Hearing the EMTs exclamation, Greg cried out to me from the front seat of the ambulance, "No Dad, No!" My first reaction was to quietly pray as I quoted the Apostles' Creed.

I was given an injection of Dilantin (an anti-seizure medication) in an effort to stabilize my condition and stop the seizure activity. The Dilantin injection stabilized me for the rest of the ride to the hospital. Even though somehow my body was betraying me, I remained conscious and strangely calm throughout the entire trip to the hospital.

The emergency room staff thoroughly examined me and subsequently admitted me to the hospital.

After enduring five days of every imaginable test, a stereotactic biopsy was performed on my brain by neurosurgeon Dr. Jeff Cole. The pathological report indicated that I had a grade three, anaplastic astrocytoma, that is a malignant brain tumor.

On July 10th, five long days after I was rushed to the hospital, I was told of my diagnosis. Reeling from the news and not wanting him to leave my doctor without getting as much information as I could, I asked the physician what the typical life expectancy was with such a diagnosis. I explained that uncertainty would be the hardest thing for me to deal with ... just the facts, please. I can handle the truth. Doctors really don't like to answer that question, but he reluctantly told me that I might live as long as three, maybe four years. Beverly and Greg were with me in the intensive care unit room as we heard the diagnosis and I could literally feel their pain as the truth of the doctor's words sank in. Andy and Ashley were in the waiting area along with my parents, brother, and additional family and friends.

Dear God, my parents.

Both of my parents had lost a sibling to cancer when they were about my age. Neither of their parents were ever the same.

My baby brother, Phil, would have to live with the same hurt that I had watched Dad and Mom endure.

My wife.

My kids.

Oh God. As I pondered the doctor's comments, I drifted away in my thoughts ... I was forty-three years old and I had lived two lifetimes' worth of experiences. Smiling at the thought of my full life, I returned to the present to address my immediate situation.

After careful consideration, I simply asked the doctor if I actually had any decision regarding my status.

Dr. Cole said yes.

I simply said to Dr. Cole, "Then ... number one, I choose to be happy, and number two, I choose to walk my daughter Ashley down the wedding aisle when she finds the man that she loves."

With a smile, I was choosing to give my all to the upcoming struggle to survive, to bravely strive with resolve to sustain dignity, honor, and diligence in what most likely would be the last fight of my life.

I would not go down without a fight to the finish. God willing, it would be on my terms.

It would be the legacy of courage and honor I would leave to my children.

The remainder of the time that I was in the hospital in Athens was very humbling for me. I never knew how many friends that I had made over the years. I never knew how much I was loved. People came from hundreds of miles away. I don't remember what anyone said, just that they came.

One particular visit meant so much to me. Paul, a Georgia State Patrolman, came to the foot of my bed while others were around me talking. He smiled at me. He stood there not saying a word for about five minutes, walked to my side, smiled, and patted me on my shoulder and left without saying a word. His presence alone spoke for him.

I was dismissed from Athens Regional Medical center on Saturday, July 13th. Because of their expertise in dealing with a diagnosis such as mine, I was referred to Emory University Hospital in Atlanta, Georgia.

While at Emory I was placed under the care of radio-oncologist Dr. Ian Crocker and neuro-oncologist Dr. Mark Gilbert. The team of physicians determined the specific protocol that would best serve my needs and I was to begin radiation and chemotherapy treatment in late July.

After being accepted into the chosen protocol, I resolved to embrace the chemotherapy and radiation as my ally, regardless of the debilitating condition to which it would render my body.

I would be thankful for their great alliance to defeat the cancer that had so rudely interrupted my life.

Under Dr. Crocker's supervision, I received thirty-three treatments of radiation concluding in early September.

I have to tell you from my standpoint as a patient, radiation on the brain isn't as bad as it sounds. They built a plaster protection device for my head, which looked and felt like a football helmet that was about a size too small when it was strapped on. On the outside of the device was a diagram that would serve as the target area for the radiation. The final radiation diagram "map" looked remarkably like a map of the state of Georgia. My son Andy suggested that I must have had "Georgia On My Mind." He always found the humor in things … God bless him, we all needed that laugh.

Each day before I went for treatment I stopped in the men's room and got down on my knees and had a little talk with Jesus, asking Him to see me through the next few minutes.

After my brief prayer, I calmly walked into the treatment room. They strapped my head in place and the technician said to me, "I'll be right back in when you're finished. There's nothing to it."

Then a 1,200-pound hydraulically-controlled door closed behind them. Nothing to it, huh?

I visualized the radiation flowing into my head as the Lord's little radioactive soldiers marching to war with the cancer that was raging in my head. I actually sang out loud the old gospel hymn *"Onward, Christian Soldiers, Marching as to War"* every time the radiation went humming into my brain. There was an audible hum during the procedure. The entire radiation treatment took only about thirty seconds to complete and then the hydraulics engaged and the door reopened.

I didn't know until all of the treatments had been completed that the radiology technicians could see and hear everything I was doing during the treatment. I wish I'd known ... I would have tried to sing a little more on key.

Upon completion of the radiation treatments, I was transferred to Dr. Gilbert's supervision under which I received eight multi-week systemic (body-wide) chemotherapy cycles. A cycle of chemotherapy lasts several weeks and is followed by weeks of rest to allow your body to regain enough strength to endure the next cycle. With calculated breaks to regain my strength in between, the complete eight cycles of chemotherapy lasted one year.

The chemotherapy followed a similar routine as the radiation, less the helmets and singing. (I still prayed in the bathroom every time.) Some of the treatments were given intravenously. Some were given orally. Fortunately, I never experienced any nausea with either the radiation or chemotherapy.

I did, however, experience exhaustion as I had never felt before. Even the smallest task seemed monumental.

Finally, after almost a year and three months of treatment, I was finished with all of the prescribed treatments and it was time to review the results. After another round of MRIs, a follow-up visit was scheduled with Dr. Gilbert.

On Tuesday, September 23, 1997, Bev and I went in to see Dr. Gilbert for the summary analysis. When Dr. Gilbert and his nurse came into the room he simply said, "Where the tumor was" ... I didn't hear another word. The treatments were successful. I asked Beverly to get all of the information and excused myself, simply saying, "I've got to call my Mama."

I am so humbly thankful to have survived this terrible disease. I don't know why I lived while others haven't.

I am so thankful to be alive.

Over fifteen years later, I am still regularly checked for any return of the cancer and continue to have positive results. My dear old friend and mentor Dr. J. W. Fanning personally advised me "to stay alive as long as you live." I continue to do exactly as he instructed even as I endure the long-term effects of having survived cancer. The radiation and chemotherapy treatments that helped save my life have also left me with degenerating joints and discs along with growing fatigue ... a small price to pay for the chance to watch your children grow up and start a life of their own as adults. As Hamilton Jordan notably said in his book about surviving cancer, "There is no such thing as a bad day."

I recently had the pleasure of sending Dr. Jeff Cole (the neurosurgeon who told me the facts about the disease that day in the Intensive Care room) a very special photograph. It was a picture of me walking Ashley down the aisle to give her to her groom, Brandon, during her wedding.

And yep ... I still choose to be happy.

"Don't Let Go ... Just Hang On!"

"A champion is someone who gets up, even when he can't."
~ Jack Dempsey

Aunt Betty buried Uncle Larry at Arlington National Cemetery in Washington, D.C. on a bright summer afternoon in 1972. He was fifty-two. He was a career soldier in the United States Army. He was my Daddy's older brother.

The previous year, Uncle Larry and Aunt Betty purchased a home in Melbourne, Florida. They were unaware of any health issues.

They planned to retire there to be near their children, who lived in the area. His sudden illness and fast decline rudely interrupted their dreams of enjoying retirement together.

Life isn't fair.

Within two years, she would lose their only son, Larry Martin, to an early, sad and tragic death.

Life isn't fair.

Even as she mourned the loss of her husband and son, her convictions drove her to be brave, have a stiff upper lip, and stand true to her role as the family's matriarch. Betty was the wife of a tough old Army Sergeant Major.

She knew what she believed.

She believed she needed to be close her family.

She believed they needed her to help them be strong.

She believed she needed them to help her be strong.

Hawaii's Military PX contacted her and offered her an opportunity to leave Maryland. She went and did the job well, enjoying tropical paradise, but ... her family beckoned her.

She wanted to be near her two oldest daughters, Judy and Trudy, who lived in Florida. She wanted to be near the grandbabies, too. After the deaths of her husband and their son, then following an escape to the majesties of the Hawaiian landscape for a brief couple of years, she decided to move to the home she and Uncle Larry had purchased in Florida.

Her youngest daughter, Betty Claire, relocated to Melbourne with her.

It was here that Aunt Betty quietly dealt with the grief of losing her husband and son.

Betty was originally from Wichita, Kansas.

She raised horses there. She loved horses.

She'd have horses in Florida.

Horses required a lot of work. That would help the time to pass. Time always heals.

Horses required a lot of love. She had a lot to give.

Her brother still lived in Kansas. He had horses and he would have the perfect horse for her.

Horses required a lot of land. She arranged to have access to the fifty acres adjacent to her property in Florida so she could enjoy having a horse.

She hitched a horse trailer to her pickup truck and headed to Kansas.

Her brother Billy did indeed have the perfect horse for her. She loaded him into the trailer and headed back to Florida, contemplating the perfect name for her perfect horse. He was a beautiful, tan-colored quarter horse. He was a large gelding who stood seventeen hands tall and weighed more than a half-ton. She would name him on the ride home.

She decided his name would be "Sir Denny."

Sir Denny proved to be exactly the right distraction Betty needed.

The harder she worked with him and his new stable mates, the more alive she felt.

The more affection she gave her horses, the more she felt restored.

Time passed.

Betty began to heal.

Her life was on the mend.

Betty shared her love of horses with her grandchildren. Grandmothers and horses are great fun for children. The grandkids were around a lot! They shared Betty's love for horses, helping her around the stables with cleaning, grooming, and feeding. Even though they were young, they learned to enjoy riding Sir Denny and his friends. They would ride in "Granny's" truck from her house down to the stable on a regular basis to be with the horses and their Granny.

The routine was always the same—feed, water, and only after the first two were done, ride. First, they must feed Sir Denny and his cohorts all the sweet feed they would eat, then lead them to the water trough so they could drink all of the water they needed. Only after the horses' needs were taken care of could you saddle them up and take them for a slow ride around Granny's farm.

One day about thirty years ago, Debbie, one of Betty's older grandchildren, and a girlfriend were over spending time with her. They went down to the stable with her to tend to the horses as usual. Debbie was about ten at the time. The girls got Sir Denny and another horse out and began the aforementioned feed and water process. Debbie and her friend were anxious to ride the horses, so instead of feeding them the sweet feed mixture that would fill them up and slow them down, they offered the horses just a handful of hay before leading them to the water trough while Betty cleaned stalls. They had the horses saddled and were on a casual trot across Betty's farm before Betty realized the girls were gone.

They made the ride trotting across the fifty-acre farm just fine, but when they turned back toward the stable the horses were hungry and ready to eat. Sir Denny broke into a full gallop and the other horse spontaneously joined him as they raced toward the stable and the delicious sweet feed they knew awaited them. Clinging desperately to the back of the two horses running over fifty miles an hour, Debbie and her friend were screaming for their lives.

Suddenly in the distance, over all the other noises, Debbie could clearly hear the old Sergeant Major's wife barking out life-saving leadership commands to her granddaughter, "DON'T LET GO … JUST HANG ON!"

Again and again and again she heard her Granny's authoritative call of assurance.

Neither Debbie nor her friend let go … they just hung on as they rode home to safety.

"DON'T LET GO … JUST HANG ON!" became something of a mantra for Aunt Betty for the rest of her life.

She fell in love some years later with a wonderful gentleman named Bill. They shared many happy years together.

Bill died after a long and complicated illness.

"DON'T LET GO … JUST HANG ON!"

Betty Claire, her youngest daughter, died after a brutal and extended illness.

"DON'T LET GO … JUST HANG ON!"

Finally, Aunt Betty had to let go … she'd simply grown too weary to hang on.

She died in May of 2007.

Debbie spoke at her memorial service. She shared the story of Sir Denny and her thrilling ride of so long ago. She told of how her Granny's command still rings in her ears and her heart.

Pausing with emotion, she remembered her Granny and how she had buried a beloved husband, a loving friend, a son, and a daughter. Parents shouldn't have to bury their children. She remembered how bravely she bore it all.

I spoke with Debbie today.

It's been over four years since Betty's death.

Even today, when Debbie encounters adversity, she still hears her Granny's call, "DON'T LET GO … JUST HANG ON!"

I can hear it too, Debbie.

I can hear it, too.

"FREE KITTENS!"

"The smallest feline is a masterpiece."
                                      ~ Leonardo da Vinci

What time is it? ... What's that noise?

The phone was ringing.

It was after midnight on a Friday night ... oh no, what's wrong?

I offered a sleepy sounding "hello" to the caller.

It was my oldest son, Greg.

Just like with any other parent, predictable words of concern came tumbling out of my mouth.

"Are you okay?"

He was fine. WHEW!

Thanking God, I breathed a sigh of relief and sleepily wondered, "Well ... what in the name of God are you doing calling at this late hour if everything is fine?"

I didn't make the comment; I just waited to hear what he had to say.

Greg enthusiastically exclaimed, "Get the kids up, Laura and I are coming home with a surprise. And hey, Daddy ... it's a big surprise for you, too."

He hung up.

His Mom and I jumped out of bed wondering what in the world the big surprise might be. With Greg it could be anything.

Greg was about to graduate from Oconee County High School near Athens. He and Laura had been dating regularly for quite a while. We speculated about his level of excitement in the call. Surely, you don't think they're coming to tell us that they're getting married after they graduate next month, do you? Oh my God …

We were completely awake now!

We woke his younger siblings, Andy and Ashley, and proclaimed their brother's intentions to surprise all of us.

We all waited for their arrival as if Santa Claus was coming.

The headlights blinded our view as they pulled into our driveway. We saw both of them get out of the car. Was Greg carrying something? Yes … Greg was carrying a big box. Something was written on the box. Yep, something in big black letters was written on every side of it. We turned on the outside floodlights as I tried to read what was written on the box.

A BIG BOX … hey, you don't announce wedding engagements carrying a big box … WHEW!

The words were becoming clear.

I could see two words written one on top of the other. In upper case bold letters was written …

FREE KITTENS!

Greg walked into the den smiling like a Cheshire cat, apparently in possession of one of its relatives.

Andy and Ashley rushed to see the kitten.

Greg gently lifted a little orange striped male tabby cat in one hand and handed him to Ashley.

Greg looked over at me with a broad smile.

He boldly winked as if to say, "Here you are Daddy … do you remember … it's your turn."

I understood.

"Free Kittens!"

When Greg was a little boy we lived out in the country, so Beverly brought home a female cat and its kittens from the vet to help with the snake and rodent population. Rodents and snakes are just a way of life around grain fields. The mama cat survived; the kittens only lived a few years. Life in the country has lots of things to use up nine lives. We had her for fourteen years before she died and the vet said she was about three years old when we got her.

Greg named the mama cat "Buffy." When he asked me how I liked the name "Buffy," I said I thought it was a perfect name for a sweet mama cat like her. With satisfaction from my comment he said, "You can name the next one."

Greg was smiling at me as he remembered the deal we'd made when he was so young.

The "next one" was here.

It was my turn to name a cat.

Naturally, he would have brought home an orange striped tabby cat … Greg was testing my recollections to the max.

Let me explain.

Several years before on a Sunday afternoon, Greg and I watched John Wayne in his Academy Award-winning role of Rooster Cogburn in the iconic cowboy movie *True Grit*. Rooster Cogburn had a roommate. His roommate just happened to be … you guessed it … an orange striped tabby cat. The cat's name was General Sterling Price. As we watched the film together, I told Greg that someday I'd like to have an orange striped tabby cat.

He remembered.

Was I looking at a potential General Sterling Price, Jr. across the room from me? That's a dang good name for a tomcat.

Names are a big deal to a cat.

T. S. Eliot declared generations ago in his classic book *Old Possum's Book of Practical Cats* (on which the musical *Cats* was based) that nothing was more important to a cat that its name. According to Eliot, allowing a person to call them by their name was the highest honor a cat could bestow upon a human.

Greg brought the kitten over and handed him to me.

He was so little. He fit in the palm of my hand.

Getting comfortable, the kitten turned around until he was curled up into a little ball in no time.

It started almost immediately … he began to purr.

This was no ordinary purr. He was loud.

It was almost like he was snoring. Do cats snore?

I laughed out loud at the content little feline going to sleep in my hand. As I listened to him purr, I said how much his purring sounded like a nine-point-nine horsepower boat motor puttering across a pond!

I did the only thing I could do.

I named him after a boat motor.

"Evinrude."

Over the next year, Evinrude rarely left my side, my lap, or my pillow as I endured round after round of chemotherapy. He was every bit as fine a roommate as Rooster Cogburn's General Sterling Price.

"Just Feed 'em Cantaloupe!"

What in the world are we going to do with a kitten?

I had four months of chemotherapy remaining when Evinrude, a baby orange striped tabby cat, arrived in the "FREE KITTENS!" box. My son rescued him in his box from a farm supply store just outside of Athens. He was the only kitten left in the box.

Evinrude was the runt. I knew how he felt. Taking chemotherapy for a cancerous brain tumor makes you feel kind of like a runt yourself. That was one thing Evinrude and I had in common.

My son, Greg, heard that a pet is good for someone who is sick.

I qualified.

I had a brain tumor. My diagnosis was made a few months before Evinrude showed up in his box.

Having now endured both of them, I can tell you that radiation and chemotherapy also have something in common, too. They cause you to feel very tired. Really, really tired. Following seven weeks of radiation, my chemotherapy treatments began. I had been taking chemo for several months before the little tomcat arrived and to say I was tired was an understatement.

I was forty-three.

My son was so proud to have brought the little fellow home to us. He was so pleased to have found him in the box. He wanted me to have an orange striped tabby tomcat from a suggestion I had made years before.

I learned a long time before, when anyone does something kind … just say, "Thank you."

Thanks, Greg.

But, what in the world are we going to do with a kitten?

All three of the kids were in school during the day. My wife went to work in the morning. The kitten's eyes had just opened. He was too young to be outside alone.

It was settled. Evinrude and I would spend all day together and we would make the best of it.

I thought I would learn to tolerate a kitten.

Evinrude thought he would steal my heart.

We learned a lot about each other.

He learned that sleeping all the time was a way of life for me because of my illness.

I learned that he loved the taste of cantaloupe.

We were very accommodating of one another's likes and needs.

I slept. I slept a lot. His favorite place to take a nap was on my belly, the warmest, softest thing he could find.

He ate. I regularly snuck him a bite of cantaloupe.

During most of the naps we took together, I would always sleep on my back.

I especially appreciated the affectionate way he told me he was ready to go to sleep on my tummy. He stretched the entire length of his foot-long length (including his tail) and expected me to wrap my hands around each of his front legs. When I did this, he stretched each leg just a little bit longer and began licking all over my hands with his little sandpaper tongue.

Time to sleep.

And sleep we did.

Over the next year, I slept with the little purring boat motor of a kitten for hours every day. It was always with the same routine, a bite of cantaloupe and the long drawn-out trip to the bed to get comfortable that ended with him stretched out on my belly, licking my hand.

I had really good, restful sleep and lots of it with my little orange pal.

Evinrude was getting big. The cantaloupe diet was really working.

He was no longer just twelve inches long.

In one short year, Evinrude now measured three feet, three inches long from the tip of his nose to the end of his tail. His weight had changed from several ounces to seventeen pounds and he wasn't fat.

And he was the runt of the litter?

God help the family who got the pick of his litter! It just goes to show you, if you want a big healthy cat ... just feed 'em cantaloupe.

When we take our daily naps now he has to lie on my ribcage. He's just too heavy for my belly. He doesn't have a clue that he's grown any over the past year. I think he believes I've shrunk.

Instead of licking my hand to fall asleep, Evinrude now reaches his right paw up until it touches my face, where he leaves it during our nap.

And while I thought I would learn to tolerate a kitten, Evinrude knew from the very beginning that he would steal my heart ... and he did.

What in the world are we going to do with a kitten?

That's not the question anymore ...

What in the world would I do without Evinrude?

Traveling Light, Wanderlust and "Muffin"

I had three months remaining with my chemotherapy treatments when Greg decided he needed to see the world. Greg was with me when the doctors told me about my brain tumor and the prognosis that I probably wouldn't live very long. For Greg, cancer meant that at the tender age of eighteen, if indeed genetics had played any part in my cancer, he calculated his life could be almost half over and he needed to get busy seeing, hearing, and experiencing everything life had to offer. He wanted to climb every mountain, fish every stream, and swim in every ocean. Time was running out and he needed to get started. I think he also just couldn't bear to watch me deteriorate and die at such a young age and needed to remember me as the strong and capable man he remembered from his childhood before I had gotten sick.

Cancer not only has a profound effect on the patient (me), but also on everyone in your life.

In his mind, Greg's formal education to this point in his life had not served him very well. He learned best by tasting, touching, seeing, hearing, and experiencing. He was a very perceptive and intelligent child and structure bored him. I could certainly relate. We both tolerated school but we certainly didn't enjoy it. College was not for him. We understood.

So, in 1997, my son Greg began his adventure.

Traveling Light, Wanderlust and "Muffin"

He left home with a trailer behind his car and tears in his eyes. His were not the only eyes filled with tears. We were devastated to see him leave, but we understood why he needed to go.

He had a plan of sorts. He would to follow his heart and the wanderlust possessing him. His first destination was Missoula, Montana. He had friends there and he could stay with them. He left with too much stuff (furniture and such), but how could we have known that traveling light would become his style?

After an eventful trip, which included several breakdowns and repairs along the way, he arrived in Montana. He gracefully fished the trout rivers of his dreams with his fly rod and reel, learned to climb mountains, and encountered wildlife in its natural element.

Greg and his friend had a close call with a grizzly bear that passed within forty or fifty feet of them near Iceberg Lake in Glacier National Park. Forty or fifty feet is not very far when you are staring down an 800-pound bear. I've never seen a grizzly bear up close in the wild (and I hope I never do) and I asked him to describe how big it was. He said that if I could imagine a large, furry bull and give it tree trunks for legs, well ... that would describe it.

Soon after, he determined that he was more concerned with a bull moose than a grizzly in the wild. He said that the stupidity and temper of the moose made it less predictable than the grizzly. His low opinion of moose was solidified even more when he got to Alaska and encountered them there. (Note to self: Stay away from angry and stupid moose, too.)

One of his other favorite activities involved "jamming" with friends on his old acoustic guitar and writing music. I remember that, as a child, he declined my offer to teach him how to play the guitar but as he watched his younger brother not only enjoy learning to play but actually learning to play quite well, he decided he would learn.

I taught him three or four chords and he took it from there. He doesn't know an A from a G, a sharp from a flat; he just knows where to put his fingers to get the sound he wants. His original song, *"Funky Biscuits,"* would become his rallying anthem as he slid through the chord progressions and growled in his husky baritone the words scrutinizing the intentions of superficial students in the college town of Missoula. Another of his songs, *"Sweet Tea in My Mouth,"* reminded him and others of his Southern roots. He was beginning to test the creative artistic soul that lay within him. He picked up work here and there to get by, but soon the wanderlust set in again and a new, bigger adventure was ahead ... Alaska.

Freshly outfitted with an adequate vehicle and supplies to make the trip, he left in pursuit of the Alaskan Highway. Unbeknownst to all but him, most of the roads were gravel throughout Canada and that only added to the adventure. If the road was not passable or just didn't take him where he wanted to go, he would just drive up the side of the mountain and meander around until he found a way to get down again.

He arrived in Denali National Park. Mt. McKinley is located there and is also known as Denali. Denali translated into English means "The Great One." The mountain is the highest peak in North America, measuring 20,320 feet tall. Greg found work in the national park that included accommodations. He climbed more mountains and saw the wildest of North American wildlife. He even went above the Arctic Circle and watched the summer solstice with the crew of ABC's "Good Morning America." He lived on Kodiak Island, at home with the largest of the Alaskan brown bears, but soon the wanderlust returned and he was off on his next adventure.

He heard that there were some really good waves on the Pacific coast of Costa Rica. Hmm, surfing? He decided to move there and learn how to surf.

He loaded up, drove his truck all the way back home, stopped for a short visit, and then caught a plane and flew to Costa Rica. He said he'd see us again when the seasons changed. He didn't say which year. He bought a surfboard, rented a cottage on the beach for next to nothing ($150 per month) and took up residence. He learned to surf from some of the locals and spent his entire summer perfecting his form. Restlessness and the desire to be back in the mountains of the West and out of the humidity and heat of the tropics led him back home. He sold his surfboard for more than he paid for it, bought a ticket, and caught a plane home to pick up his truck and say hello before heading west again.

He arrived back home, caught up on visits with all of his relatives, and then was off again. With his truck and camper loaded with love and best wishes, he headed back to the mountains of the Northwest that would become his home.

He spent that autumn searching for a place to winter. He called me from his cell phone one evening while suspended under the craggy rock-lined summit of one of the "Three Sisters"— three volcanoes, each peak exceeding 10,000 feet in height, located in the Cascade Range in Oregon. He called just to tell me that the sun was setting and he was gazing into the distance at the Pacific Ocean when he saw that he had a signal on his cell phone and thought he'd call me to say hello and let me know that he was happy.

I cherish the memory of that call. How do you top that?

He later sent me a picture of himself starring into the wilderness of the Bitterroot Mountain Range from the summit of Trapper Mountain with a note that said, "Every time you look at this picture of me, know that at this moment, I am completely happy." The picture resides on a bookshelf where I see it every day.

I didn't hear from him again for another three months, when one afternoon he called with an important question. "Hey Dad, what's the difference between a sea lion and a seal?" No small talk, no how are you, just a question. I simply responded, about 500 pounds and not much else, to which he replied, "Cool, I think I've made friends with a sea lion that lives on a big rock out here in the Pacific Ocean." He went on to explain that he was in the city of Trinidad in Humboldt County, along the Pacific coast in the very northern part of California, nestled right next to Oregon. He had gone there to explore the giant redwood forests.

He had been staying there for a couple of weeks in a state park that bordered the Pacific, living out of his truck's camper. He … just parked his truck in a lot adjacent to California's legendary coastal Highway 101 and took up residence. Each morning he walked down to the Ocean to have his "wake up, chilly bath for the day." Uninvited, Greg made his way onto this particular sea lion's rock that just happened to be the easiest point of entry for his swim in the Pacific. When I say rock, I mean a really big rock. Greg described the rock as about the size of a house. The rock was covered with smaller seals, which always scattered into the ocean with Greg's approach. Not the sea lion. The sea lion always made a show of charging toward Greg and making sure that he was jumping into the ocean instead of staking a claim on its rock. By this time, Greg was accustomed to wildlife encounters (the grizzly bear, bull moose, etc.), so he wasn't too concerned about the sea lion actually challenging him if he just kept moving and jumped into the ocean.

Well, on this particular day the sea lion dove into the water, following Greg, and then swam up close to him almost to the point of what seemed a friendly encounter. He described the animal under water as being as graceful as a bird in flight. In just a few more days, their swim together became a morning ritual.

Across the street from the lot where Greg was camping was a solitary commercial structure. One morning, as the weather was getting colder, a gentleman strolled across the street and spoke to Greg. He had noticed Greg's Georgia license plates and wanted to caution him. He said that he had seen him befriend the sea lion and wanted to tell him that just in case he didn't know, the waters are regular feeding grounds for great white sharks and they feed mainly on seals and similar species. The cold waters there are abundant with the giant predators. Greg thanked him, offered him a cup of coffee and introduced himself and described the adventures that had led him there. The gentleman returned the pleasantries and returned to work.

His name was Muffin and he was an artist.

The next day Muffin returned with a couple cups of coffee and invited Greg into his studio. Muffin was a glassblower. Curious, Greg accepted his offer and Muffin showed him his studio and explained about his art. Muffin asked Greg how long he planned on staying in Trinidad. Greg explained that he was thinking of staying in the state park across the street through the winter, that his best pal was a nameless sea lion, and that he loved the redwood forests.

A few more days passed and Muffin returned with a proposition.

He and his wife had talked about the guy from Georgia who was friends with a sea lion and he knew that winter would be rough in a camper and that maybe Greg would like to consider spending the winter nights in their studio. The furnaces for glassblowing were always hot and their studio would provide a warm place for him to rest. In return, Muffin suggested that maybe Greg could sweep up the place before retiring. It was settled at last ... Greg would spend the winter along the Northern California coast in a glassblowing artist's studio.

Over the next four or five months Greg not only "swept up," he also stayed during the day and watched Muffin blow glass. Watching Muffin work, Greg discovered the dormant artist in himself. His exposure to the creative artists in their studio awakened a desire to learn how to blow glass and explore his own creative capacities. As the winter progressed, Muffin sensed his interest and asked Greg if he would like to try and do some of the preparatory work required to produce basic glass art. Greg readily agreed and Muffin gained a new apprentice.

Greg spent the next couple of years studying with Muffin there in Trinidad.

The studio prospered. All of the art they could create was sold and Greg's skill continued to improve. One day Muffin, like the mother bird that encourages the chick from the nest, suggested to Greg that he had all of the skills necessary to open his own studio. Muffin had more business than he could handle and he was beginning to decline business. He could send

Greg all of the business he needed to help him launch his career as an artist. Greg's passion for glassblowing had become his profession.

Greg arranged to purchase all of the equipment and supplies needed to open his studio.

He located his studio in the artist's haven of Ashland, Oregon, about 200 miles to the north of Trinidad. He began his own operation around nine or ten years ago. He now successfully operates "Blue Mind Designs – Flame Work Design in Glass." Like Muffin, he has served as a mentor to apprentice artists who remain associated with the studio, and many have gained renown for their work as well.

I have never met Muffin. I don't even know his name. Yet, I will always hold him in a special place in my heart for reaching out to a brave, happy wanderer full of dreams and wanderlust, and seeing the artist within.

God bless you, Muffin.

From the tears of his departure to the subtle smiles of the wisdom gained from being true to himself along his journey, Greg has found his place.

He is happy.

"Somebody Bet on the Gray"

"I bet my money on a bob-tailed nag, somebody bet on the gray!"
~ Stephen Foster

It was a Sunday afternoon in April 1997.

I was watching New Zealand golfer Frank Nobilo win the Greater Greensboro Open when the commercial aired. "The 123rd running of the Kentucky Derby, next Saturday live on NBC, starting at five o'clock Eastern time."

Hmm . . .

Nine months earlier, I had been diagnosed with a cancerous brain tumor. The pathology report actually called it a grade three anaplastic astrocytoma. In layman's terms, I had an inoperable cancerous brain tumor the size of an egg in my head. According to my doctors, I had a very limited amount of time left to live. (I'm writing this fifteen years later so I am still very much alive, but I didn't know that I would be so fortunate at the time.)

After pausing to daydream about it a moment, I thought ... why not?

I went to ask my wife, Bev, if she wanted to go with me to the Kentucky Derby on the following Saturday. She said that as much as she would like to go, she couldn't even think about it with church commitments and so little notice. She was the church pianist and they depended on her for the services. Naturally, I understood about prior commitments. I walked back into the bedroom to watch golf again.

The more I thought about the race the more curious I became about the chances of going. I had never seen a horse race, much less The Kentucky Derby. I could at least give them a call and check on tickets, right? I owed that much to the legendary sportswriter of my hometown newspaper *The Atlanta Journal-Constitution*, Furman Bisher. Secretariat, Seattle Slew, Affirmed—all Triple Crown-winning horses when I was a young man—had been brought to life for me by his words.

I mustered up all of the Southern charm I could and called Churchill Downs to request tickets. After the ticket agent, Eileen, toyed with me for a few minutes she graciously explained that all of the reserved tickets were sold months in advance and that none were available. With a chuckle, I explained why this might be my last chance to see a Derby. She understood. I said that I'd be coming anyway. I told her that I'd look her up at the ticket window when I got to Louisville the next Saturday afternoon.

I left on Friday in my old blue Ford pickup truck and drove until dark. I saw a sign for Mammoth Cave National Park, Kentucky. I exited and drove into the park to see if they had accommodations available. I stayed at the hotel in the park. It rained hard all night. The next morning, I got up and dressed for the Derby in my jeans, multi-colored windbreaker jacket, a pair of cowboy boots, and a "Hunt's Oyster Bar" baseball cap.

I visited the Mammoth Cave as rain continued to fall. I've got to tell you, that cave was a heck of a sight. The guide explained how we should not remove any rocks from the cave; yes, I have a souvenir rock from the cave in a drawer somewhere.

On the way the rain began to fall harder. I had been a little sick before I left home. I was still taking chemotherapy for the brain cancer, so I thought it would be wise to find a place to buy a poncho and maybe get a lawn chair. If I was indeed able to get close to the outside of the track, I wanted to stay dry if I could and I didn't want to have to sit on the wet ground or stand up all day.

As I neared Louisville, there were dozens of signs to the track. I drove around until I saw the most advantageous place to park that allowed for an easy exit after the race. A group of Boy Scouts and their leader were allowing folks to park in the local Methodist church's front yard. Perfect, you could drive right over the curb and back onto the street for a hasty getaway. Plus, I've always been a sucker for a kid in the rain and it was pretty close to the racetrack. I put my poncho on over my jacket, grabbed my lawn chair, and was off to the races.

As I approached Churchill Downs, I realized I was farther from it than I had previously thought. This place was huge. I made it to a side entrance ticket window where for about a hundred dollars you could get inside the track on a wet, muddy infield with a lot of folks who were feeling no pain and watch the race on a giant screen while all the time resembling the crowd of Woodstock back in August of 1969.

I opted to continue on to the front gate and the main ticket window.

When I arrived at the front gate, I introduced myself to the ticket attendant and asked for Eileen. I told him that I'd promised to tell her hello. Eileen wasn't on the grounds. Explaining as I did the previous weekend to Eileen that this would probably be the last chance for me to watch the Derby in person, the attendant compassionately listened. After he courteously told me that there were no tickets available for purchase for this years' race, I asked the ticket attendant where the best place would be to put my chair to take in the sights through the fence from outside the gate.

He looked me over one last time and smiling, said, "Just let me keep your chair for you. Just go in, see the horses in their paddocks, the betting windows, some of the patrons, just enjoy your time here and stay as long as you'd like."

I handed him my chair.

I was in Churchill Downs!

I looked at all of the horses. I considered placing a bet. I watched the people dressed in their finery getting equally as wet as me with my jeans, cowboy boots, and baseball cap from my favorite place in the world to eat raw oysters.

I felt so lucky to be there.

I saw an older guy sitting on a bench near the windows where you placed your bets.

He was dressed in a Peter Falk detective character "Columbo"-styled trench coat with a newspaper boy cap perched atop his head at an angle. He was chewing an unlit cigar and studying some sort of pamphlet. I took a seat next to him and asked him how to place a bet. Not only did he explain—in a distinct Northern accent—the details involved in placing a bet, he also assured me that I should take a horse named Silver Charm to win. I did.

I placed a three-dollar bet on Silver Charm to win.

My next goal was to try to get close enough to see the track. I simply kept walking in the direction that everyone else was and lo and behold, there it was, the track itself. There appeared to be a large tunnel underneath the track that continued farther into the stadium. Most people weren't going that way, so I decided that it was the way for me to go. On the other side of the tunnel I exited and was funneled to an area of seats right beside the track on the inside rail of the track near the finish line.

No one was sitting in these seats. Hmm.

A Kentucky State Patrolman stood in his rain gear beside the entrance to the empty seats. I stopped and talked to him as the rain continued to fall and my poncho and baseball cap kept me dry. We talked of the weather and such and I told him that I thought I'd better grab one of the empty seats while they were still plentiful. He didn't seem to mind and I was thankful. I sat as near to the finish line as possible about ten rows up. I couldn't believe it. I watched two preliminary races and didn't move a muscle. I had never seen anything as exciting as sitting close to the track as the horses galloped past. How could I be sitting where I was? Why weren't there any more people in the stands? I thought it was sold out. Was it because of the rain? Regardless, I wasn't moving unless somebody insisted.

And then it happened.

A lone trumpet sounded a call in the distance and just like in a cartoon, 150,000 people descended into their seats like thundering hogs answering a dinner bell. I was clearly out of place with all of the fashion statements surrounding me and was waiting for the patrolman to come and show me the way out when another man in a raincoat leaned over to me and whispered, "Seats forty-five and forty-six on this row will not be occupied today." I looked at my seat. I was in seat number fifty. I moved four seats down and turned to thank my anonymous advisor, but he was gone. The University of Louisville band was just beginning to play Stephen Foster's *"My Old Kentucky Home."* Soaked and smiling, I sang along.

In what seemed like seconds, the race begun and I experienced the most exciting two minutes of my life.

When the race was run and the blanket made of 554 red roses was presented, it laid across the shoulders of none other than the beautiful gray horse, Silver Charm. I left the grandstands and headed to the window where I had placed my bet to see how much my winning would total. On the way, I thought that maybe I should just keep the winning ticket as a memento of my adventure, but when I was told of the amount my three-dollar wager had become, I simply asked for directions to the souvenir shop.

On the wall in the room in which I am sitting hangs a small, vibrantly-colored Leroy Neiman print of the "Derby Day Paddock," subtitled "123rd Kentucky Derby, Churchill Downs, May 3, 1997." It's my lone souvenir.

To the anonymous authors of my day—the gentleman at the ticket window who allowed me inside the grounds to take a look, the old grizzled gambler who insisted that I place a bet on the eventual winner, the Kentucky State Patrolman who allowed me to take a seat on the finish line, and the man who allowed me to keep a seat by suggesting that I move four seats down—my thanks to each of you.

It was all like a dream.

As I left the Churchill Downs souvenir shop, I walked back by the ticket counter. The same attendant was there and he had my chair for me as he had promised. As he reached to give it to me he asked if I had a good day at the track. I responded with thanks and told him of my adventure.

He smiled, winked at me, and said, "I'll be sure to tell Eileen."

A Multi-Colored Yellow Jacket

"Failure at some point in your life is inevitable, but giving up is unforgivable."

~ Jean Finnegan Biden

My son Andy applied and was accepted to Georgia Southern University during his senior year of high school in 2001.

Also during the winter and spring of that year, I had to have multiple joints replaced within a six-month period. The degeneration in my joints, a side effect from the chemotherapy I had taken five years earlier as I battled cancer, had advanced to the point that I could no longer use my arms and legs effectively and was in constant pain.

Dr. James Andrews in Birmingham, Alabama replaced both of my shoulders and both of my knees and assured me that although the pain would go away, the extent to which I could use my new joints would depend on me. Lots and lots of physical therapy was my immediate future. As I worked to regain my mobility, Andy was a diligent coach, entertaining me, encouraging me, and pushing me to my limits. Today, I still reap the benefits of his devotion and encouragement. My son proved to be a great coach and a very able leader.

He was elected "Class Clown" of his senior class, an honor that fit him to a tee. You have never met a more happy-go-lucky kid. He was the epitome of a free spirit. He was a very talented and quietly driven young man.

He learned to play the guitar while he was in middle school. As I was traveling on business in South Georgia, I stopped by a music store in Baxley. Wandering through the array of instruments while waiting to see the owner about advertising, I thought I might call my sons to see if they might have an interest in learning how to play the guitar. I could strum a few songs myself and thought I could show them how to do the same. Might be fun. Greg had no interest at the time but Andy declared that he would love to learn how to play.

I bought Andy a guitar and we had fun stumbling through the basics. A couple years later, we could play *"Dueling Banjos"* together. There wasn't anything else that I could teach him. Andy had learned every song I knew and was hungry for more. He downloaded guitar tablature for song after song and mastered it all.

I sure enjoyed watching Andy enjoy playing his guitar.

What I didn't realize at the time was that his peers did not share my enthusiasm as he was learning to play. They were not very patient with his learning curve and razzed him as he struggled to learn. Doing their best to discourage him, they unwittingly strengthened his resolve to learn to play.

Andy would not stop.

He would play the guitar and play it well. Soon the fuzzy notes became clear and the chord progressions began to sound like songs we knew. Soon his friends were asking him to play for them. Soon they were asking him to teach them to play as well.

Andy was asked along with some of his friends to play the class song, *"Forever Young"* by Bob Dylan, for their high school graduation ceremony. The unmistakable windmill arm-action style of The Who guitarist Peter Townsend has never been more perfectly duplicated than Andy playing and entertaining at his graduation. Amid the cheers and applause at the performance in Stegeman Coliseum at the University of Georgia, I couldn't have been more proud of him.

After the graduation ceremony, I met his buddies in the crowd and listened to them tell stories about how they gave him hell when he was learning to play. "Just look at him now," they said. They were proud of him too. I even heard one of his teachers say (while smiling and shaking his head back and forth), "Oh, that Andy Brown." Andy had stolen the show.

This persistent dedication to overcome adversity by learning to play the guitar well while in the presence of teenaged ridicule was to prove a precursor of things to come.

Andy and I drove to Statesboro together to get him settled in the dorm for the fall semester at Georgia Southern. We listened to The Beatles' *White Album* (isn't it great when your kids like the same music that you do?) the entire trip, quietly enjoying one another's company one last time before he began this new stage of his life. Being together on the 200-mile ride to Georgia Southern was nice. His mom and sister were coming later with more of his stuff so I got to enjoy the time alone with him.

The following morning, we helped Andy move all of his things into his dorm room. It was then we met his new roommate, Lawrence Dantzler, IV. We weren't there an hour before Andy had nicknamed him "Big L." Big L was from Macon, and he planned to study business at Georgia Southern. Then he planned to go to culinary school and become an executive chef. Here was a young man who knew what he wanted to do and how he was going to do it. After taking the new roommates to lunch and going on a shopping spree for groceries, we left them to investigate and get settled into their new home together.

Andy enjoyed every second at Georgia Southern both in (he had excelled in an art course) and out of class ... well, mostly out of class. His grades were a fair reflection of his extra-curricular activities. Andy struggled with the responsibilities of independence without the discipline of home. So did I thirty years prior. He didn't develop the correct discipline it took to attend class and study until a few years later. Uh ... me either. Does anybody not have trouble with that? I know I did. On the social scene he struggled to learn that moderation was the key to behavior at a party and that infatuations didn't equal love. Okay, okay, enough of this ... so did I.

At the end of the first year, having failed a few courses along the way, he had earned a grade point average of D. Having been a student with similar results myself—that is, I had more expertise outside the class than in—I had no issue when he asked (well, maybe begged) to return for his second year.

He pledged to do the necessary things to raise his grades and he did exactly as he promised. At the end of the second year, he had raised his grade point average to a D+.

He had decided that he only had the capacity to make incremental steps unless he changed his environment. Again, he pledged to improve his efforts as he changed his setting. Leaving Georgia Southern to Big L, Andy transferred to Georgia Perimeter College, a suburban Atlanta two-year college.

He attended that summer semester and true to his word, he worked hard and finished with an A grade point average. He registered for one more semester. At the completion of his second semester his grade point average was still an A. During his two semesters at Perimeter College, Andy had earned his way onto the Dean's List twice (something that I never did).

After two successful semesters at Perimeter, Andy decided to apply to Georgia State University. He would lobby for admission based on the improvement in his GPA from his first, second, and third years of study from Georgia Southern and Georgia Perimeter. After humbly pleading his case to the Georgia State University registrar and pledging to continue improvement of his GPA, the registrar mercifully granted him entrance.

Andy was accepted to Georgia State and began his studies in math. Andy proved worthy of the task. He finished his first semester with an A average and he made the Dean's List. More importantly, one of his professors encouraged him to believe that he had an aptitude for aspects of architecture. He encouraged Andy to consider exploring the opportunity of making a transfer application to Georgia Tech. Andy was enthused by the professor's faith in his ability and began to work harder than ever.

We constantly talked of his dream of becoming a "Yellow Jacket." Andy had become a man with a plan of his own.

The results of his second semester at Georgia State were a mirror image of his first semester. Andy made A's in every area of study. During the third semester, with the continuing encouragement of the math professors at Georgia State, he began the process of application to Georgia Tech. While he worked hard at Georgia State, he interviewed with several Georgia Tech alumni seeking their endorsement of his application. He finished the third semester at Georgia State with all A's again and awaited word from the Georgia Tech admissions department.

I was in charge of a remote operation for our company in Carrollton, Georgia, when the call came. While sitting at my desk late one afternoon, Andy told me that he had been accepted for admission into Georgia Tech. When I hung up the phone, I sat at my desk and wept for joy at the dedication of my child's efforts being recognized and rewarded.

Three years later, on a cold, rainy morning in March, Andy graduated *cum laude* from Georgia Tech with a degree in Building Construction. He is successfully employed with a global construction company as a project engineer. Yep, Andy is a *"Ramblin' Wreck from Georgia Tech and a Helluva Engineer"!*

In attendance at his graduation ceremony was a beautiful young architecture student with whom he had studied at Georgia Tech. Rebecca had completely swept Andy off his feet. They were head-over-heels in love.

On August 8, 2009, Andy married Rebecca in a pristine garden. Big L, who is now the executive chef at his own restaurant in his hometown of Macon, stood by his side as his Best Man.

Dreams do come true.

There wasn't a dry eye in the house.

The Third Time was the Charm

Danny and Jake were born four years to the day following my first seizure. That seizure was the first indication of the malignant cancerous tumor growing in my brain. The doctors said I might have three, possibly four years to live.

Yet four years to the day later, I stood in the hospital with my sister-in-law, Tamra, and my brother, Phil, waiting together on the birth of their twin boys, Danny and Jake.

Tears of joy flowed like a river.

All of them were mine.

Phil gently asked if I was okay ... I had never been more okay.

I was going to be an uncle ... "Uncle Dave."

Phil is the brother you want if you have children.

He adores all three of my kids. His love is tireless. His devotion is unquestionable.

He was only twenty-one when Greg was born. Phil thought Greg was a new pet and he treated him just like one. Can you love a pet too much? Phil didn't think so.

When Andy was born, Phil was twenty-five and just beginning to understand that you can't throw kids as high as possible and then catch them every time. Andy adored Phil. He and Greg couldn't wait to be together with Phil. They had such fun.

The Third Time was the Charm

By the time Ashley was born, Phil had reached the advanced age of twenty-nine and with all his vast experience as the fun uncle, he just assumed Ashley was going to adore him as much as her older brothers. However, Ashley was born with a woman's intuition that told her that Phil was not to be trusted. As hard as Phil tried to get her to fall in love with him ... Ashley stubbornly refused.

And then Phil married Tamra.

Tamra became the conduit that allowed Phil into Ashley's heart. Ashley decided he must be okay if Tamra loved him. Phil was euphoric at Ashley's acceptance.

Tamra and Phil love my kids like they were their own.

Tamra would sit on the floor with each of the children playing board games, working puzzles, explaining how to make things using origami paper folding and any other quiet activity that interested them. She was as "patient as Job" as she enjoyed the intimacy of their interactions.

Phil, on the other hand, was a regular "Wild Man of Borneo." No Monopoly games for him. It was "Hey, Uncle Phil ... let's pull the trampoline over next to the house and then you jump off of the second story and see how far you bounce, okay?"

Together they were the ideal aunt and uncle to my kids.

They would be wonderful parents.

All of my family was excited at the prospect of little "Phils" and "Tamras" running around in diapers.

When the time was right, their family would bloom and grow ... all in good time, all in good time.

Mother Nature didn't cooperate with Tamra and Phil when they decided it was time to start a family. After consulting the doctor, they learned that Tamra would not able to conceive a child in the traditional manner and they would need to consider other options.

Tamra and Phil had come to a crossroads. They could adopt or they could consider other medical options.

They decided they would pursue the medical option of in vitro fertilization.

Hopeful they would soon be parents, they proceeded with their first attempt at in vitro fertilization. Following the procedure they waited patiently for the results ... failure.

Disappointment.

"If at first you don't succeed ... try, try again!"

After the second procedure, again they waited ... failure.

Heartbreak.

' ... Try, try again!"

For the third and what had to be the final time, they underwent the difficult procedure again and again they waited ... SUCCESS!

The third time was the charm!

Danny and Jake were born on July 5, 2000.

I was almost forty-eight and for the first time in my life, I was an uncle.

After having survived a cancerous brain tumor, I realized the likelihood of ever pulling a trampoline over next to the house and then jumping off of the second story to see how far I could bounce for Danny and Jake would be a stretch for this brand new "old" uncle.

I had some really big shoes to fill in my new role as an uncle.

I was following a legendary uncle.

This would require thought.

After some contemplation, I decided to just be myself. It would have to be good enough. After all, I am a compilation of all of the influences in my life and there were some really good ones ... two came to mind.

Uncle "H" was the most fun relative I've ever known. We were buddies. He never let up in his pursuit of cracking me up with a joke, a gesture, a roll of the eyes, or scaring the hell out of me on a regular basis. He was simply telling me with his actions, rather than his words, that he loved me.

Daddy's baby sister's husband, Uncle Charlie (outside of my immediate family), was the most generous relative I've ever known. Although he never was very good at the game, his hobby and his passion was golf. I think sometimes he lived vicariously through me every time I made a birdie putt or had a hole-in-one. He gave me golf club after golf club. He always said he'd tried to play with them but he thought they'd suit my game better than his. Just as with Uncle "H," he too was telling me he loved me.

Hmmm.

Filling the role that Uncle "H" played for me with Danny and Jake wouldn't be hard. We would laugh and play together ... albeit not on a trampoline. Filling the role that Uncle Charlie played for me, however, would take time and cultivation.

But, I had an idea.

I collect Case pocketknives.

I've got a couple hundred of them in display cases scattered around the house. They're kind of like jewelry for a country boy. Trust me, they are. I've carried a pocketknife in my pocket just like my PaPa and Uncle "H" did since I was a kid.

I would give Danny and Jake a Case pocketknife for their birthday and Christmas presents from now on. They'll get the first one July 5, 2000. No better time than the present, huh?

Maybe someday they'll get a kick out of the memory of an uncle who thought they would enjoy collecting Case pocketknives as much as he did. As I started their collection, I hoped the cancer in my brain would stay away long enough for us to get to know and love one another. Thank God ... it has.

Danny and Jake just celebrated their tenth birthdays.

Just a couple of days following their tenth birthday, Phil called me on a Saturday morning and said that the boys had asked if they could bring their shoeboxes of pocketknives over to my house and have me tell them all about them. He said their interest and curiosity about them was beginning to grow.

The three of them came over and we spread a towel across the kitchen table and one by one we discussed the details of each of their pocketknives.

Each of their collections has reached twenty-one Case knives ... so far. We talked about them together for hours.

I love my nephews. I love being their "Uncle Dave."

Except for them, I'm not their "Uncle Dave," I'm their "Uncle Doo" ... and that is another story altogether.

The Road Back

"Birds sing after a storm. Why can't we?"
~ Rose Fitzgerald Kennedy

Divorce . . . Failure . . . Pain.
Change.
Time . . . Healing . . . Strength . . . Hope.
Blessings . . . Happiness.

Have you ever hit "bottom" and realized "it ain't pretty"?

Have you ever wished that you could turn back the clock?

Have you ever had thoughts and actions you regret?

Have you ever lived with secrets in your life that smothered you and clouded your willingness to act on your beliefs?

Have you ever justified your behavior as "just trying to be normal"?

Have you ever tried so hard to please everybody that you successfully managed to not please anybody?

Have you ever had your personal shortcomings exposed to all those that you care about? Heck . . . have you ever had your personal failures exposed to people that you don't even remember how or why you even knew them?

Have you ever felt so disappointed in yourself that you couldn't even verbalize it?

Have you ever been too ashamed to confide of your need for help with those you love?

Have you ever been too embarrassed to even go to church?

Have you ever even managed to think that in spite of all of the things happening to you, your ego still wants to believe that you can find a way to fix everything?

Have you ever wished that there were no repercussions or consequences for your actions?

Have you ever wished you weren't about to become another statistic?

Have you ever realized that sometimes it's best just to accept failure?

Have you ever been completely humiliated?

Have you ever wished you could erase painful memories?

Have you ever wanted a second chance?

Have you ever longed for renewed hope?

Have you ever wanted to be forgiven?

Have you ever been through a checklist similar to the one above and still managed to have a smile on your face?

(. . . Pausing to take a <u>DEEP</u> breath . . .)

Well, I've survived some pretty hairy stuff … mid-life terminal brain cancer, sixteen surgeries in the past twenty years, an innocent, youthfully-inspired financial flop … and the answer to the last question in the above list is . . .

With a simple faith in an unseen God, whom through grace could love even me, I (along with plenty of others) have made it through with a smile on my face.

It was a close call for me. If it were not for a simple gesture of a phone call from a son on an Easter afternoon . . . well, I shudder at the thought of how sad I had become.

Thank God.

Going through a divorce is the most painful thing that I have ever experienced.

My divorce occurred after twenty-eight years of marriage.

I can "fancy up" the words to construct a menagerie of fluff. But, in the end, regardless of the old adage of there being two sides to every story . . . I hold myself accountable for the failure of my marriage.

Nonetheless, having failed . . . I still can make the best of my failure.

Divorce is a failure. Failure, especially in "matters of the heart," hurts so deeply. To consider divorce anything other than a failure is to set myself up to be the victim of my own self-deception.

It made me feel disposable.

It brought heartbreak and devastation to all of the people involved.

Change was required.

Change requires time.

Today, Beverly and I are happily remarried to others. I thank God that Ron came into Beverly's life. I thank God that Sheri came into mine. Beverly and I are so fortunate; these two wonderful people became our second chances.

Second chances are always welcome.

Speaking for myself, today I need and desire the discipline of commitment.

While certain desires may be healthy and normal, in my experience that cannot be said about undisciplined desires . . . it cannot be said of those desires that willingly reject the difficulties that can be required for a dedicated commitment.

To understand and willingly desire to bear the difficulties, as well as the joys that such a commitment requires, gives me strength to move into the future with Sheri.

Even though my first marriage failed, I need this belief for my second one.

Time allows for healing.

Healing regenerates strength.

And as an old Southern gospel hymn so eloquently suggests in a portion of its final verse:

"… strength for today and bright hope for tomorrow,

blessings all mine, with ten thousand beside!"
Strength ...
Hope ...
Blessings ...
Happiness.

So ... You Don't Think You'd Miss a Cat?

"What greater gift than the love of a cat?"
~ Charles Dickens

Because of divorce, my tomcat Evinrude and I won't be roommates any more.

Make no mistake, Evinrude was my cat ... well, okay, I actually belonged to him.

Nobody owns a cat.

The orange striped tabby and I had a helluva run together for five years. I probably could've asked for him, but the inside of our house was the only home he'd ever known. I didn't have the heart to ask when I left home if Evinrude could come with me. My daughter was still at home.

I wouldn't do that to either of them.

So, you don't think you'd miss a cat?

You would.

I wasn't even a "cat person" and I sure did.

Thoughts of when my son Greg brought him home in the "FREE KITTENS!" box.

The memories of him purring and sounding like a boat motor, then naming him "Evinrude."

… Of our unspoken alliance forged with one another as I was recovering from cancer. Our loyalties were based on nothing other than simply touching each other.

… About the time it snowed four or five inches. We thought we should see if Evinrude liked it. He didn't. We gently placed him in the snow outside of our front door. From a standing position he leaped about ten feet straight through the open door to the warmth of the house. Not a drop of snow leopard in his DNA.

… How he'd become so big. The crazy cat's first year's growth was to the size of a bobcat. Of course he didn't understand why he couldn't sit on the soft part of my belly anymore. Eventually he settled for me holding him upside down, cradled in the nook of my elbow scratching his tummy … for years.

Yep, I missed Evinrude.

Thinking about it made me sad.

When my daughter told me that he'd been given the old heave ho out of the house and into the yard … well, it broke my heart.

He'd always been an indoor cat.

He'd had a not so subtle, extended disagreement with his current landlord over certain bathroom privileges. According to my daughter he pled his case well, but he wound up living outside. He remembered the floor plan of the house. He knew which window to find. He wouldn't give up that easily. Evinrude jumped into my daughter's bedroom window and sang a mournfully sad blues ballad about dying alone in a gutter. I'd taught him the song years before. Perched in her window he growled it out every night … he got her attention.

She snuck him into her room.

He secretly slept there every night until she left for college.

The first winter she was gone, he slept with the dogs in their doghouse; the next summer he slept with the dogs in their doghouse.

Before you knew it, my daughter was married and moved away. She came and got her dogs.

Fed and provided fresh water regularly, Evinrude remained outside ... alone.

Fortunately during their years together, he and the dogs had dug tunnels all over the yard. After the kids went on a trip to Boston the tunnels became known as "The Big Dig." The Big Dig was a series of tunnels the dogs and Evinrude dug underneath the barn in our back yard. The tunnels allowed him to be cooler in the summer and warmer in the winter. He had an insulated doghouse for an above-ground retreat, but it was indeed a "dog" house and a cat has his pride.

Evinrude was now alone ... for years.

I rarely heard anything of him except from my children.

On visits home and during the holidays, the kids would always give me detailed reports on my old friend. Like how the summer sun bleaches his orange striped fur a golden yellow and how he's developed a taste for fresh squirrel.

Great God Almighty, my old lap cat had become a predator.

Just doing what comes naturally, I suppose. I have a hard time visualizing him killing; although, we had plenty of wrestling matches when I thought he considered killing my hand.

As years passed, he was evidently getting a lot of exercise and had actually trimmed a couple of pounds according to all of the kids.

He sounded as though he had adapted to his changed conditions very well.

After I was married again, Sheri and her kids heard all of the legends of Evinrude and his escapades. Everything you have read and more. There's not enough room to write what a crazy character he is on these few lines. You have to experience something like Evinrude. Independent, affectionate (on his terms) ... he even has verbal names for different people, announces desires, moods, and that's just the beginning. He's different.

It has been six years since we were roommates.

He was eleven in April 2008. What a great cat. What a great pal.

Whenever I think about him it always makes me smile.
I always wanted an orange striped tabby cat.

"Somewhere Over the Rainbow" ... is a Cabin at Big Canoe

"There's a land that I dreamed of, once in a lullaby."
— Yip Harburg

I was a renegade entrepreneur for decades when an old friend from the corporate side of the advertising and publishing industry reminded me one day at a conference that he "liked my style." We talked about the future.

Heck, I didn't even know I had a style ... so naturally, I was flattered. I spent most of my time putting out the endless everyday "fires" of the small businessperson and making payroll every two weeks. He was well aware of the cancer in my recent past and still wanted to bring me into his enterprise and offered me a piece of his much larger business.

My old friend ran a two-billion dollar enterprise owned by an even bigger enterprise across the Atlantic, a multinational conglomerate. Again, I was flattered and humbled.

After a few months' consideration of the generous opportunity offered to me, I chose to leave the comforts and struggles of owning my own business. When you are in business for yourself, you are always signing the front of the check and hardly ever thinking about anything for yourself. I was looking forward to endorsing the back of the check for a change. Life as an entrepreneur had been very fun and rewarding, but ... I really was looking forward to endorsing a check from someone other than myself.

Nice change.

The relocation would bring me home to Atlanta, where I had lived until I left for college about a thousand years prior. I'd be back in familiar areas, around old friends and most importantly, closer to most of my family.

Nicer change.

Single at the time, I bunked with Mama and Daddy in a room over their garage for about a year as I looked for just the right place to live. We had a blast living together. I quickly acclimated to the corporate environment and the regular fourteen or fifteen hour days. Mama, Daddy, and I enjoyed being in the loving confines of our family home again.

I found a local church that was perfect for me and got involved. The church was large enough to be lost in the congregation, but I also found a kind and caring small group of single folks about my age in the Sunday school program. Socially, I didn't care if I ever had another date ... all I wanted to do was love my kids, indulge myself with my parents, my brother and his family, reacquaint myself with all of my aunts, uncles, and cousins, be involved in a church and ... see if I could still get it done in a large business environment.

Nicest change.

On the weekends I looked for a place to live.

After the wonderful year I spent with my folks smack dab in the middle of my "one-hundred year lifespan" plan, I moved into my new home in Big Canoe. Big Canoe is a mountain community development about an hour away from my other home ... the office.

I called it "The Shack."

A better "man cave" never existed. Being a hermit on the weekend became my motivation throughout the week. It was forty-seven miles to the office. I left early and beat the inbound Atlanta traffic and returned late when there was no traffic.

When I was home at "The Shack" on the weekends it felt like I was a million miles away.

Just getting there made me relax. As I entered the development every evening I had an "Aah" moment ... the temperature was ten degrees cooler, my blood pressure automatically dropped to one-twenty over eighty, my heart rate decreased, my breathing slowed, my senses sharpened. I rolled down the windows or opened the sunroof to see and smell all of the mountain flora and fauna. More times than not, I encountered bear, deer, turkeys, or raccoons standing in the serpentine asphalt lane that led three miles past three clear lakes, rolling waterfalls, golf courses, indoor and outdoor tennis courts, a gym, an indoor pool, and (get this...) a "Little Brown Church in the Wildwood" that led me home.

"The Shack" sits under a shady canopy of mature hardwood trees. It has distant mountain views from three different sides of the house.

You never have to lock the door ... just walk right in.

"The Shack" has covered porches on the front and back of the house. The front porch is open all the way across the house and filled with rocking chairs and swings. The roofs of the porches are metal so you look forward to it raining to listen to an original symphony from the raindrops every time.

Out back is a screened porch scattered with soft furniture just perfect for a Saturday afternoon nap. Adirondack chairs are lined across the open deck overlooking the mountain-view and there's a Weber grill conveniently located at the end of the deck. Perfect. Just perfect.

"The Shack" is all wood, inside and out, except the fireplace in the den, which is made of stacked stone about twenty feet tall. I've built fires in it in the middle of the summer. There are a couple of bedrooms on the main floor. I guess you'd call them master suites ... and a ton of places for people to sleep upstairs. The inside of the whole place looks kind of like a Longhorn Steakhouse ... except I don't think I've ever seen a moose on the wall at Longhorn's.

I have three skinny artificial Christmas trees with white lights on them in the den, too ... four, five, and six foot tall trees; they stand year-round right in the middle of the front window. I turn on the lights Thanksgiving night and turn 'em off on New Year's Day. I just like the way they look standing there the rest of the year. Easiest Christmas decorating I've ever done.

Hey ... I told you it was a guy kind of place.

But, the best part of the whole house is that there are two places in the den where I can reach my remote for the cable TV and still fall asleep comfortably either for an afternoon or an entire night ... the red leather recliner and the buffalo plaid couch.

A recliner, a cushy sofa, the remote control, and cable TV ... perfect, what a place to come and crash.

Clicking her heels as the movie *The Wizard of Oz* is ending, Dorothy could've never said it better ...

"There's no place like home. There's no place like home."

Good night, Auntie Em ... wherever you are.

Denominations, Autumn Leaves, and the "Group Dynamic"

"Daddy grew up as an Episcopalian ... what a great word for a kid."
— Dave Brown

When I moved up to "The Shack" in the mountains of Big Canoe, I started going to the "Little Brown Church in the Wildwood" just around the bend from my cabin nearly every Sunday morning.

Okay ... two, maybe three Sundays out of four is probably more realistic.

This was the first interdenominational church I ever consistently attended. I enjoyed the congregation. We sang the same hymns, read from the same Bible, and the preacher preached about the same Jesus. All things considered, I didn't see too much difference from the churches with which I'd become accustomed.

The congregation seemed more intimate because of the smaller number of people and the smaller, beautifully rustic chapel where they worshipped. After all, we were each other's neighbors in Big Canoe. I was too tired after my typical seventy-hour work week to be any more involved than just attending the worship service ... okay, maybe I was just too lazy ... who knows? Anyway, I didn't get involved in a small group as I had at the previous church in Atlanta ... and for now, I liked the "Little Brown Church" just fine.

Growing up, everybody I knew was a Baptist, a Methodist, or either a "we need to keep them in our prayers." I never knew why ... still don't. I'd heard of all the rest of the denominations. However, I didn't actually know anybody who was member of another one until I was grown.

Especially "Episcopalians" (great word for a kid) ...

I found out from my Granny "Bim" that Daddy grew up in the Episcopal Church and sang in the boys' choir back home in Connecticut. She said he got paid a quarter to sing every Sunday. Imagine that ... my Daddy, a paid professional singer as a child. Good grief, he might've been another Jackie Cooper, "Spanky" McFarland, or Macaulay Culkin, who knows? I wonder why he never told us ... his mother always said he had the purest soprano voice.

Maybe it's because my brother, Phil, and I both had our voices change when we went through puberty between the ages of two and three ... both of us would be basses in the church choir today except that Phil can't sing worth a damn ... ask anybody who knows him. It's just a God awful monotone warble ... like a muffler with a hole in it.

I wonder if Daddy ever shared this tidbit of soprano fame with any of his fellow WWII foxhole buddies ... just asking.

While I missed the fellowship and time with the members of the previous adult singles' Sunday school "gang" in Atlanta, I did not miss the commute that would have been required to maintain a consistent relationship with them. I did subscribe to their class email broadcast and I regularly read about their activities during my absence. Most of the names were familiar, some were gone, some were new ... it was just good to stay in touch, even if it was just electronically.

In Big Canoe there are about 2,500 homes scattered amongst eight different mountains. Roughly one third of the homes are occupied full-time by either retirees or people who work locally, the second third are for fellow Atlanta commuters like me, and the last third are second, third, or fourth homes to people scattered like the four winds with a different primary residence or are rental properties for others to come and enjoy.

One of my fellow members of the singles' Sunday school class in Atlanta happened to have a second home in the development a couple mountains further into the property. She had the home a couple years prior to my acquiring "The Shack." Thus, we were neighbors and occasionally saw one another for coffee or dinner on the weekend. I was always kindly included in any class updates and invited to return anytime. I always felt welcome and still felt like I was a member of the class as a result.

I received a call from my former classmate late one Monday night in September and she proposed that the two of us offer to host an autumn "enjoy the color of the leaves" weekend for our old class on the first weekend in November (the traditional "peak weekend" for fall color) at our homes in Big Canoe. An organizing effort had already been made and she assured them of my willingness to see the old "gang" for a weekend to be sufficient cause for me to become a partner in the festivities.

It was a solid, safe group of people. We were just there to enjoy one another's fellowship. No hanky panky foolishness. The class's "group dynamic," although sometimes lopsided to one gender, provided an overall comfortable environment for the majority of the class members.

Like the New Year's Eve a couple years prior when the gender equation was imbalanced yet the group dynamic ruled ... I, along with another Dave, showed up for dinner. Dave had to leave and be with his kids before the party barely started. While completely understandable for the other Dave to have to leave, the group dynamic mandated that I go out dancing and shooting darts with about a dozen ladies ... all good Methodists, mind you. Well, I went, shot darts, and danced until my replacement knees were squeaking ... all in the name of the group dynamic. But I must confess, after all was said and done, midnight on New Year's Eve was kind of fun even if it was with about a dozen good Methodist ladies. Enough said, maybe the group dynamic ain't such a bad thing.

Anyway, back to the "enjoy the color of the leaves" weekend. Declining her proposal not really being an option ... I still made a futile effort to drive a hard bargain ... I asked for details of my expected "peak weekend" responsibilities.

It was explained to me that my total involvement would be to host a pizza party on Friday night (they would reimburse me for the cost of the pizza), drive the pontoon boat around the lake on Saturday, and finally, make available every possible sleeping arrangement I could within "The Shack" for the weekend.

Not bad.

She would do the same at her house and host all of the food preparation and consumption after Friday.

Not bad, not bad at all.

Heck, maybe some of 'em might be game for coming with me to the "Little Brown Church in the Wildwood" for a taste of my newfound interdenominational adventures?

There'll be hiking, fishing, golfing, boating, and a bunch of middle-aged stupid team-building games with plenty of good food, fun, and fellowship.

Plus, I'll be sleeping in my own bed.

Hmm ... nope, not too bad, not too bad at all.

Okay, decision made ... I'm in.

I guess I'd better find that vacuum cleaner I haven't seen in a couple years.

After all ... what could come from a harmless little autumn leaf-watchers weekend?

"Now, THIS is What a Mountain Cabin is Supposed to Look Like!"

"Flattery will get you everywhere."
~ Mae West

Friday, November 5, 2004 ...

This is the day that the "old gang" from my old adult singles' Sunday school class in Atlanta arrives for the autumn leaf weekend together.

I just needed to be a good host for a couple of days and then they would all be gone by Sunday afternoon. Some planned to attend the 10:30 Sunday morning worship service at the "Little Brown Church in the Wildwood" and enjoy the buffet down at the golf course dining room before their departure.

All of this was great, especially their early Sunday departure.

On Monday, November 8th, I had to open a market for the company a couple hundred miles away at eight o'clock in the morning and oversee a marketing "kick off" with a couple dozen people in attendance. I needed to be there Sunday night to prepare for their arrival.

Two days later on Wednesday, November 10th, I was to be in Asheville, North Carolina at the Grove Park Inn for a company leadership conference for the remainder of the week.

To put it mildly, I was very preoccupied with my responsibilities at work.

Why couldn't the leaf weekend have happened any other weekend than this?

Oh yeah, this was gonna be "peak weekend" for fall colors ... please, Lord, just let it go smoothly and don't let anyone sense my preoccupations while I am a co-host for so many good folks at my home.

Oh, why couldn't this have been any other weekend?

My neighbor and fellow Sunday school class member, Mary, was co-hosting at her home in Big Canoe, as well as coordinating the entire event. She had given me the logistics of the weekend and the names of the people who would be staying with me in my cabin, hmm ... quite a few names that I didn't recognize ... new friends maybe?

I could only hope so. These were really nice folks.

As the first event of the weekend, a pizza dinner followed by homemade desserts was to happen at my place. Directions to get there would be absolutely necessary. Back then, in 2004, *MapQuest, Google Maps,* and portable GPS weren't quite as precise with the southern tips of the Appalachian Mountains as they are today.

The directions went out via every possible way at the beginning of the last week of October. This included directions from our old church in Atlanta to Big Canoe, and then the trickiest part ... directions from the Big Canoe entrance to my front door. I included very descriptive and concise maneuvers to guide folks throughout the curvy, sometimes confusing and winding roads of the area where I lived.

Everyone was supposed to arrive by five o'clock Friday afternoon and only a very few would be arriving later, but the route was very dark, poorly lighted, and could be especially confusing at night.

As I completed the set of directions to forward to all of our guests, I closed it with the explanation of my potential dilemma at work, which might very well cause me to arrive late to the very event that I was hosting.

I also confessed that my doors were never locked and welcomed them to just go in and feel at home should they arrive before me.

Finally, I described that my multi-colored Christmas lights would be blaring their atypical glow from the back side of my cabin down into the valley below so that they could see them on their approach. I closed just like yesteryear's and current Motel 6 advertising spokesperson Tom Bodett … "Come on in! I'll leave the lights on for you!"

Then I busted my fanny to get everything done in advance to be ready for my corporate responsibilities, as well as my personal obligation to help Mary and the Sunday school class to have the best possible time together. By the middle of the week, everything was ready … professionally and personally.

AHHHHHHHHHHHHH …

I would be able to thoroughly enjoy my guests and leisurely manage my leadership responsibilities for the next week's business activities.

On Friday morning, I went to the office early. After having a leisurely lunch with three of my close associates, I left midday for Big Canoe. I got home in time to relax, take a nap, wind down from the intensity of the week, and do a few last-minute things to make sure the cabin was ready for the arrival of my guests.

The leaves were turning colors exactly on schedule for the weekend. A few were beginning to fall. I thought that I'd blow the leaves off the porches and driveway before the people started to arrive. I moved my car down the street to a neighbor's driveway since they wouldn't be here this weekend and I knew we'd probably need all the room we could get for everyone at my place. I was in a pair of shorts and actually worked up a sweat as I spruced up outside to make the place look nice. Outside lights on, door open, Christmas lights glowing from the back porch down into the valley below, I was as ready as I was ever gonna be … time for a shower.

I stepped into my bedroom, took off my shirt, kicked off my shoes, and was standing there in my shorts when I looked to my right and there in the hall stood Rhea (pronounced "Ray") smiling at me!

I offered a fond hello to her as she was asking me, "What are you doing here?" HA! She hadn't seen my car in the driveway and by the nature of my directions she did exactly as she was told and just came on in. Rhea would've just come on in anyway; she is just that spunky and comfortable with herself. A delightful and gregarious lady.

I assumed she was by herself until I heard these resounding words echo from the vaulted ceiling of my den ...

"Now, THIS is what a mountain cabin is supposed to look like!"

The voice that exclaimed the engaging approval of my cabin was one or two octaves higher than nearly any woman's voice I had ever heard ... almost like a girl.

I stepped shirtless and barefooted around the corner to see who had uttered such flattering words about my cabin. She, like Rhea, hadn't expected for me to be here. She broke into a big smile and started infectious laughter as I said, "Hi, I'm Dave, welcome to the cabin!" Rhea introduced her, "Dave, this is Sheri Knight."

How fun! How nice! What a great way to start the weekend! I excused myself from Rhea and Sheri to take my shower and urged each of them to make themselves at home. Having showered, shaved, and changed into some clean jeans and a flannel shirt, I reappeared to host any others that may have arrived during my absence.

Nobody else was here yet so I just sat down with Rhea and Sheri to visit.

Rhea stood up in front of the fireplace and, smiling a coy smile with hands on hips, offered the following suggestion, "Dave, my boys would love this place ... so, I say to heck with the class's group dynamic. Let's get married."

That's Rhea ... I was flattered. Sheri laughed out loud.

Nobody else has ever asked me to get married ... Ever.

I smiled, looked at Rhea and simply said, "Well, I'll tell ya,' Rhea, I'm flattered but you don't want to marry me. I'm living up here completely content with everything I'll ever need. I have a good relationship with the

Lord. All I really want to do is love my kids, indulge myself with my parents, get a little more involved with my new church, spend some more time with my brother getting to know his family, and ... see if I can still get it done in a corporate business environment. But heck, Rhea, thanks a lot!"

She smiled, winked, and said fair enough.

Sheri, sitting to my left on the other end of the couch from me, said, "Gosh that sounds a lot like me."

I turned to her and inquisitively asked ... "Really? What size shoe do you wear?" (The ladies of the class had a running joke about me being interested in someone only if their foot would fit into an imaginary glass slipper.)

Suddenly, before Sheri could respond ... the doorbell rang.

Restoration

"Then the light of my blessing will shine on you like the rising sun."
~ Isaiah 58:8 (NIRV)

If I make the phone call, I will be violating the secret unacknowledged code.

The single adult Sunday school class's legendary "group dynamic."

The group dynamic is an unofficial, unwritten, and unspoken rule. While the class does not frown upon interaction between prospective couples ... there remains a wariness of ... well, let's just leave it at "interaction between prospective couples" having the potential to affect the very important group dynamic of the "old gang" of the singles' Sunday school class in Atlanta.

The weekend has finally ended. It was a roaring success. Everyone has finally departed and I am left alone ... content again with my peaceful solitude.

Except for today, I have these tingly magic feelings.

Anyway, so what about making the phone call?

It all began a couple days before with the first of the guests' arrival. Rhea surprised me just as I was about to take a shower. She brought her friend Sheri, a new class member. Having showered, I assumed my role of weekend host and after politely declining Rhea's proposal of marriage (she really liked my cabin), I became more interested in making Sheri's acquaintance.

Could her voice really be as tiny and high-pitched as it sounded or were my ears playing tricks on me? Just as we were beginning our first conversation, the doorbell rang ... and the weekend was off to the races.

Having only had a brief moment to converse with Sheri before the other guests arrived, I wanted to learn more. Sheri had made one comment regarding something I said and all I inquisitively asked her was, "Really? What size shoe do you wear?"

I wanted to continue the conversation.

Strange, I felt like Ray Walston's character in the old '60s sitcom *My Favorite Martian.* It was like a pair of completely unfamiliar antennae came out of my head seeking a signal.

Strange feeling ... a very strange feeling ... maybe the strangest feeling I've ever had (not to be melodramatic, but for the love of God ... have you ever felt like you had a pair of imaginary antennae coming out of your head, seeking a signal?)!

A little voice said, "Continue the conversation with her, David ... or put the pair of really weird-looking antennae back in your head."

Continue the conversation ... ?

How?

When?

Where?

For crying out loud ... about WHAT?

And what the heck was that tingly, goofy feeling that hit me like a ton of bricks?

Had my imaginary antennae received a "ping" in reply?

Did she have a set of antennae, too?

Was she a Martian?

Did she feel the "tingly feeling"?

Sheri and I only spoke one sentence.

What was that feeling?

Shake it off, Dave, shake it off, you have guests arriving. People were beginning to come in throngs. I retracted my imaginary antennae and went to work on welcoming my guests. And arrive they did. By the time they'd stopped arriving there was a crowd of around two dozen.

Fun!

My responsibility for the first night was to get enough pizza for the crowd.

I took the other "Dave" (there are two of us) from the class with me to get pizza at a local restaurant. Just making conversation, on our way the other Dave casually asked me where I met women at a remote place like Big Canoe.

I had to level with him. I'd never met a woman anywhere at Big Canoe. While I'd met a lot of wildlife, I hadn't met any of that kind of "wild life." I wouldn't have the first clue where to do so. Just never really cared about it.

However, I did mention on the ride that earlier, before the others started to arrive, I briefly met Sheri and she seemed very nice. (I didn't say a word about antennae.)

The other Dave endorsed her with verve.

He explained that she had the two most wonderful children.

Hmmm, kids ... cool. I love children, always have ... they can see through a line of "baloney" a mile away. They know if you really care. They rarely tolerate a phony. Kids shoot straight. I love that.

He told me that Sheri had a boy named Jason who was thirteen years old and a little girl named Jennifer who was eleven. Cool ... really cool.

Continue the conversation with Sheri, David.

Upon our return to the cabin with the pizza, the ladies had taken over my kitchen.

A really big red bowl filled with fresh salad was on the kitchen bar, flanked on either side by an array of homemade desserts.

LOOK ... somebody had baked a homemade white chocolate raspberry cheesecake.

Somebody bless the food, it's time to eat!

Hmmm, look at that big red bowl. Having inspected the big red bowl as it sat on the kitchen bar, I secretly wished that whoever brought it might forget to take it home with them when they left Sunday.

I liked the big red bowl.

It looked good on the bar in the kitchen.

Time for dessert and I knew what I was having … a slice of that surreal looking homemade white chocolate raspberry cheesecake. When I made my request, the slice of cheesecake arrived smothered in raspberry sauce.

I didn't care how it tasted … it was a visual masterpiece.

I placed my fork on the cheesecake and with one smooth swipe the bite was in my mouth being savored for what seemed minutes. I wondered aloud who made this delicate and delicious morsel.

Smiling as she waved at me from a distance, Sheri's tiny and high-pitched voice said, "Me!"

Continue the conversation for crying out loud, David. She can cook!

After playing some crazy games, it was time for all of us to go to the appointed places to sleep. Mary, my co-host, has a house in Big Canoe too. The rest of the meals would be at her house. She coordinated the sleeping arrangements. We would split for the night and gather back together at Mary's Saturday morning for breakfast.

After a good night's rest, the folks that stayed at my cabin were ready to eat on Saturday morning. As we were leaving for Mary's house the phone rang. Caller I.D. indicated it was Mary's number calling. I answered, expecting Mary.

It was a growingly familiar tiny, high-pitched voice. "Hi Dave" came her response to my hello. "This is Sheri. I left my big red bowl on the bar and I need it to serve breakfast. Could you bring it with you when y'all come?"

The big red bowl … was hers.

Continue the conversation, David. She's got good taste.

After breakfast there were options for everyone—golf, boating, fishing, hiking, shopping, napping, reading, and just hanging around Mary's house or my cabin being lazy.

My assignment was to drive the pontoon boat around the lake a couple hours, enjoying the leaves' changing colors. Eight or ten of us decided to take the leisurely cruise. As we loaded into the boat for the ride, everyone sat on the left side of the boat. It was a natural thing to do, since that's where most of the good seats are. I was the only one on the right side.

Pulling into the main channel of the lake, I was about to ask if just one person could shift to the right side to counter our imbalance, when someone stood and moved. Sheri walked to the very front right corner, leaned against the railing of the boat and it was perfectly level.

I couldn't continue the conversation with her.

She was too far away ... standing right in my line of sight.

I did notice she was wearing a brown cowl neck sweater. I did notice she had long blond hair that shined against a deep blue sky and the beautiful changing colors of the mountain hardwoods in November. I did notice that when she turned to flip her hair out of her face without touching it with her hand, all of it moved and curled around her neck and one shoulder ... for two hours.

Driving the boat that day wasn't a tough assignment, I'll tell ya'.

That afternoon at Mary's house I finally sat down with Sheri at the dining room table. The sun shone brightly in her face and I was poised to resume the conversation of the previous afternoon when I looked into her eyes.

All that I could manage to say was, "Wow, did you know that your right eye is two totally different colors?" She laughed and responded, "The blue is my real eye color and the brown part is a freckle."

Before another word was said, one of our friends walked up and sat down.

Sheri smiled at me and then winked! She winked at me. How fun, a flirt!

The conversation had been continued.

After supper Saturday night, all of us wandered around Mary's expansive house. At varied times numbers of us sat on her screened porch where the fireplace held the glowing embers of a hot fire. I enjoyed its warmth. I was getting tired.

I was sitting on the porch alone enjoying the fire as the back door opened.

It was Sheri.

She sat on an adjacent rocking chair. We had a nice talk. She answered my inquisitive "Really?" and laughingly answered the other question from the prior afternoon. We were both business professionals. She was younger than me and still had her kids at home. She was totally devoted to them. I asked her to tell me about them. She asked me and I told her about mine. She suggested that the next time I had some time in Atlanta to call her and we could meet for a cup of coffee.

I couldn't have been more pleased with the suggestion!

We joined the others for another crazy game.

On Sunday morning about half of the folks had gone home to Atlanta. Mary and I were taking the remaining half to the morning worship service at "The Little Brown Church in the Wildwood," Big Canoe's interdenominational church. We would eat lunch together at the country club before everyone left for home.

Following lunch, several folks came back by my cabin to have one last look. Sheri and Rhea were there. Sheri took a post-it note and wrote her phone number on it. She discreetly slipped it into my hand as they were leaving.

Evidently she knew about the group dynamic, too.

Two hours later I'm holding the phone.

Let's see, I'm not a member of the Sunday school class in Atlanta anymore.

I go to church in Big Canoe at "The Little Brown Church in the Wildwood."

The group dynamic is fading fast … I'm calling.

I dialed.

Sheri answered. She'd just dropped Rhea at home. She'd taken a wrong turn on the way home. We laughed. We reviewed the weekend. We talked for an hour.

We talked Monday, Tuesday, Wednesday, Thursday, and Friday.

When we talked on Friday she invited me to come and have a cup of coffee the next afternoon. I would pick her up at her house around 4:00 Saturday afternoon. The kids were to be away, her son on church activities, her daughter having dinner with her dad.

When I arrived I was surprised to meet her kids.

It was a delight.

Jennifer made a quick and observant assessment when she inquired candidly to Sheri, "Mom, how old is he?" I was fifty-two. Sheri later explained that I was the oldest guy that she had ever dated. Nice, wisdom only comes with experience, right?

Jason and I had a good conversation and decided a card game shouldn't be out of the question for later.

What a happy home. What beautiful kids.

The day ran long and we decided to have dinner together instead of coffee. I invited the children. They politely declined. Not only good kids, but smart kids.

We ate at an intimate local steakhouse.

We talked for hours.

Both of us were transparent with one another. How refreshing. Honesty is such a liberating trait. By the end of our meal, without speaking, we knew that this felt very special.

It was just the beginning … we were falling in love.

That crazy feeling was back again … what was it? We talked about it and Sheri said that when we were in "The Little Brown Church in the Wildwood" she suddenly had a passing tingly magic feeling. She said that her initial thought was … where in the world did that come from?

We had another date the following weekend.

We were falling more in love.

The "feeling" was getting stronger. We both had it, we discussed it, and FINALLY we both knew what it was ...

Someone, somewhere was helping us to find each other.

We had faith ... God was providing.

Those tingly magic feelings were the good Lord restoring us.

We spent lots of time together with her children. They knew we were smiling all the time ... they recognized our happiness. They enjoyed it.

She met my kids at the cabin in Big Canoe. We all spent time together. We laughed together. They saw how happy we made each other.

Our kids know their parents. They sensed the sparks flying. Heck, my daughter Ashley asked Sheri if she could marry her if I didn't and Jennifer reconciled my age issue. Wisdom ruled. Jason and I had our card game.

We fell more in love.

Those tingly magic feelings were the good Lord restoring us.

We met each other's parents in December.

She invited me to her family's Christmas dinner. My parents came to meet her at the Christmas Eve service at the old church in Atlanta.

Both sets of parents knew their children. They knew sparks were flying. All were happy for us. Her mother assured her it was okay.

We fell more in love.

Those tingly magic feelings were the good Lord restoring us.

Sheri and I seriously dated for the entire year.

We fell more in love.

On Christmas afternoon the following year, standing together on the bridge at the top of Amicalola Falls overlooking Big Canoe, I got down on my knee and asked her if she would be my wife. She said, "Yes!"

We were married a month later in "The Little Brown Church in the Wildwood," just as the tingly magic feeling told Sheri we would the first time she ever walked into the building two Novembers ago.

Happiness together as one big family ... for me, there is no substitute.

We all are falling more in love with each other every day!

Those tingly magic feelings were the good Lord restoring us.

Fast forward ... Sheri and I celebrated our fifth wedding anniversary on January 22, 2011.

Every day with her gets sweeter. She's the most wonderful thing that's ever happened to me.

Those tingly magic feelings were the good Lord restoring us.

And by the way, in case you didn't know ... God has a sense of humor. Sheri always said, according to many of her friends, "I'll never get married again unless God drops a man on my front door step!"

Dear God ... Thank you for dropping Sheri on my front door step. Amen.

Our "old gang" of friends from the Sunday school class thinks that we are one of the class's sweetest stories!

"Tingly magic feelings" always trump "group dynamics."

And if you just have to know ... she wears a size nine and it fits in the imaginary glass slipper like a glove!

"Cosmo" and "Pinky"

Sheri is the happiest person I've ever met.

It doesn't surprise me that she quickly became the brightest spot in my life.

What I wasn't prepared for was my acceptance into her wonderful family.

Their acceptance has been both a welcome and humbling experience. What a surprise it's been to feel so loved at this stage of my life. What a delight to have in-laws who clearly loved me, in-laws who clearly welcomed my love as they claimed me ... as theirs.

After I met Sheri's kids the first time, I couldn't wait to get to know them.

I met Jason quite unexpectedly the first time I went to Sheri's house.

He was away on a church youth retreat and Sheri was to pick him up from church when he called. Sheri and I were sitting in her living room getting to know one another when Jason walked into the room. The youth group had arrived back to the church early and he caught a ride home with a neighbor.

Surprised to see an unfamiliar man in the house, he looked me over, grabbed a chair across the room, moved it close, spun it around, and sat down. We talked for about an hour and a half. He told us about the church outing he'd attended. He asked me if I knew how to play Texas Hold 'Em. I confessed that I wasn't sure if I did or not, but I'd like to learn. He asked … when Sheri and I finished whatever it was we had planned, would I like for him to teach me.

Of course I would!

With no poker chips in the house, we substituted a box of plastic spoons. Using the den ottoman for a table we sat and played Texas Hold 'Em. Naturally, he beat me right down to my last spoon.

Later, we had a rousing round of lemon bowling. Lemon bowling, you ask? All you need is the kitchen floor for the bowling alley, water bottles for the bowling pins, and lemons for the bowling balls. We had a blast.

He was five feet, six inches tall and just barely a teenager.

Jason was always tinkering with something, seeing how it ran or why it didn't. He just couldn't stand not taking something apart and putting it back together again. Watching him patiently work at solving problems, he reminded me of a little wizard. I nicknamed him "Cosmo," sometimes shortened to "Coz." It stuck. Sounded like a bright young wizard's name to me.

A few years later, during his high school graduation, Sheri and my kids decided to honor Jason's selection of Auburn University as his college of choice. His sister Jennifer, stepsister Ashley, stepbrother Andy, and Andy's wife, Rebecca dressed up as Auburn Tigers and painted across their bodies, "Congratulations, Cosmo!" Grinning with his unmistakable broad smile at all of the "tiger" celebrants, he quietly nodded his approval from his position in the processional.

They all adore one another.

Today, he's six feet, five inches tall and beginning his fourth year at Auburn. He's such a fine young man.

Last week, Coz called me. It was his first day of class. When I said hello, he said, "Konnichiwa, Dave. Ogenki desu ka?" He's taking Japanese this semester and was showing off his new-found ability from his first day of class to tell someone hello and ask them how they are doing.

He was smiling.

So was I.

"Cosmo" and "Pinky"

I met Jennifer the same day I met Jason.

She came to the door, checked me out, and turned to her mom and whispered something. From Jennifer's quick, frank, and correct pre-teen assessment of me to her mother ("Mom, how old is he?") to my emotional preparation for her graduation from Northview High School tomorrow, it's been like a Walt Disney "wish upon a star" dream to have been able to love this child.

She was an adorably secure little girl about to get braces for the second time. She was very creative, clearly had a passion for art, and sang all the time.

I will never forget a trip Sheri and I made with her, taking her to see her cousins in South Georgia. We became stranded behind a traffic accident for six hours. The road was closed. It was April. We rolled down the windows and patiently waited for the accident to clear. We made up silly songs. We ate everything in the car.

And then ... about four hours into our wait as she sat behind me, I felt her touching my ear and then messing with my hair.

I could barely breathe.

I closed my eyes and whispered a prayer, "Oh, thank you dear Lord for letting me feel affection from this beautiful child. Amen."

I reached my hand behind my back towards her finger as she was investigating my thinning hair. She met it with a quick flick ... she was in control here.

You couldn't have chiseled the grin off my face with a jackhammer.

Sassy little thing!

Although today she would categorically deny it, Jennifer loved anything pink. Everything she wore the first couple of years after we met was pink. Just like everyone else that I love, I gave her a nickname. I nicknamed her "Pinky." Sometimes, I shortened it to "Pink." It stuck. People know her name is Jennifer; they also know that her stepdaddy loved her enough to give her a special nickname. Most folks in my family lovingly refer to her as Pinky or Pink all the time. She picked out the shirt she wanted me to wear to her graduation tomorrow night earlier today … yep, you guessed it … it's pink.

Pinky was in my son Andy and daughter-in-law Rebecca's wedding. She was one of Rebecca's bridesmaids.

My daughter Ashley considers Pinky her baby sister. She can offer no higher compliment.

She is a beautiful young woman. She's such a good girl. She's so smart. She loves to cook. She's ready to take life by the horns. She still sings all the time.

She leaves for college in a couple of months.

We'll be empty nesters.

Both of these wonderful kids have been like the icing on life's cake. Jennifer wants the icing to be pink. So do I.

How will I ever explain their being gone to my sweet tooth?

Back Home Again with Evinrude

"Love me, feed me, never leave me."
~ Garfield, *Garfield: The Movie*, 2004

It was lunchtime. Sheri and I were sitting in the sunroom watching it rain on a cold November morning of 2008 when my son Andy called. He sounded concerned. He'd taken his fiancée, Rebecca, to visit his mom and during their visit he began feeling sorry for our old pal Evinrude being stuck outdoors in this weather.

He was rambling on and on about my old pet tomcat being alone all of the time outside in the elements. "Winter is coming, Daddy. Evinrude is getting old. He's not getting enough to eat. It's raining and he's just sitting out in the rain," he ranted.

I figured he might be trying to justify taking Evinrude home and letting him live with him.

"Have you spoken with your mom about this?"

"She's traveling a lot with work."

"Andy, I'm sure he's being fed well. I'm sure he's safe. Maybe the old boy is just getting old. After all, he was eleven in April. Talk about it with your mom. If it's okay with her, why don't you just take him home and see how he likes it?"

"ME? I can't take him home! ... I already have a cat and two dogs!

"I was thinking *you* would like to have him. Daddy, he really looks weak and I've already talked with her. He's a burden for her. Sometimes, when she's out of town, she has to come a long way just to leave food outside in the feeder for him …"

Sheri has ears like satellite dishes; uh, well … they don't look like satellite dishes … let's just say she has excellent hearing. I wear hearing aids that are always turned up as loud as they will go. I had the volume on the phone on high while I was talking to Andy. So even sitting across the room, Sheri heard the conversation and with a wave of her hand to get my attention, she silently mouthed the words, "Just tell them to bring him here."

"Are you sure?" I mouthed back to her. "I thought you were allergic to cats." She just smiled at me and thought, for better or worse … as she said, "They have allergy medicines." She loved cats. She just hadn't had one in years. Neither had I and I missed the one we were talking about.

What a gal!

As Andy continued to plead Evinrude's case, I interrupted him and quickly said, "If you're sure it's okay with your mom, just put him in the car and y'all bring him to our house."

Silence.

"Say that again, Daddy."

I did.

He said okay and quickly hung up the phone.

My old tomcat was coming home.

I hadn't seen Evinrude in years. I wonder if he'll recognize me.

Andy called a couple times during the hour ride from Athens to Atlanta. They'd taken him indoors and given him a bath (the dang crazy cat loves warm water and can swim like a fish), blew him dry, stopped at the pet store and bought him a new collar. They were clearly excited to be bringing him here.

Evinrude arrived late that afternoon.

When Andy brought him in the back door, the old cat looked at me and made the identical sound he'd labeled me with so many years before. It sounds like a twirling tongue rolling an extended "r" in Spanish, then ending the twirl with "WOW"! Well, for cryin' out loud ... he recognized me!

Andy heard it, laughed, and handed the old cat to me. I turned him over on his back, laid him in the angle of my left elbow, and scratched his tummy just like old times.

Evinrude will be just fine.

He didn't look a bit skinny to me.

Somehow ... I knew he probably wouldn't.

All our kids have tender hearts. This was just another example. Andy just couldn't let Evinrude spend another winter outside.

Before the week was over, Evinrude named everyone else in the house with a very own unique meow. We gave him the run of the house. He was, after all, eleven years old and experienced in so many ways of life now.

He settled on several chairs that my wife regularly occupies. It was as though the cat knew she was the one who offered the official invitation. By his insistent and constant affections towards her, he has never let Sheri forget how much he loves her for letting him come and live with us. He is always angling for a spot in her lap. Always.

When I took him to meet the vet for the first time, I gave the vet the complete oral history of Evinrude and me. The doctor said that he was in the prime of his life. He would most likely live another five, seven, maybe even nine years. The brown spots on his gums were typical for an orange striped tabby as he grew older. Otherwise, Evinrude was the picture of health. Thirty-nine inches long and fifteen pounds of the loudest purring cat he'd ever met. The vet's only instructions were that it would probably be good for Evinrude to lose a pound or two. (Laughing to myself, I could hear Andy's plea that he was not getting enough to eat!) I explained that he would be giving up his fresh squirrel by remaining indoors and the vet said that would probably be the only diet change he would need.

Almost three years have passed since his return home. He was fourteen this past April. He weighs thirteen pounds and he has a few more brown spots on his gums.

Evinrude is asleep, wrapped around my shoulders as I write this in the sunroom.

This is his house.

He is content and so am I.

My good old orange striped tabby cat is back home with me to stay.

"Oreo" ... not the Nabisco Cookie

"You think dogs will not go to heaven? I tell you, they will be there long before any of us."

~ Robert Louis Stevenson

His name is "Oreo." I've only known this wonderful dog for six years. He was eight and a half when we met. It was love at first lick. There were lots and lots of licks. His father was a Border Collie and his mother was a Springer Spaniel; the stout result of their union is a bastion of my new family. He has ably served them for over fourteen years ... as noble and loyal a dog as I have ever known.

When I asked for Sheri's hand in marriage, he was included in the roll call of approvals that I knew I must receive for me to proceed with any plans that involved her. When I explained to Oreo my intentions he simply wagged his tail and approvingly did his Oreo "dance," where he raises both front feet in a syncopated rhythm while bouncing to and fro. I was relieved at having gained his enthusiastic approval.

Oreo, needless to say, is a very special pet. All of us are his responsibility. He is in charge. He will do anything necessary to make sure we are safe. What a noble creature.

I have had other special pets.

"Freckles" was my first dog when I was a kid.

"Daisy" was the kids' first dog.

"Doodlebug," a stray dog that just showed up at the house one day, vicariously became the neighborhood's first dog.

"Evinrude," a big orange tomcat, still lives in our house because he wants to. I don't think a cat belongs to anyone; they consider themselves above such a trifling concept. We love him, too.

All have come and gone except the cat. He's planning to live forever and probably will.

A wise minister named Felix offered consolation following an accident that took the life of another dog from my innocent young adult life, a little gray Schnauzer named "Pepper." As I sought comfort for my loss, Felix simply said to me that he hoped again to see the beloved pets of his life someday, somewhere.

I have never forgotten his words.

I am glad those words of solace are with me tonight. Wherever life has taken you, Felix, I humbly whisper a thank you for your influence.

I knew the time would come. I hoped that it wouldn't.

Oreo began losing his hearing about eighteen months ago and over the past year has become totally deaf. He has begun to slip, stumble, and sometimes fall when he is out and about in the yard just being a dog. The falling has increased and it has been harder and harder for him to get up.

When I went downstairs to feed him yesterday morning, Oreo wasn't able to stand by himself. The stout legs, the oversized paws, the broad shoulders, the heavily muscled frame, just won't support his weight anymore. He looked up lovingly, longingly with those big brown eyes as to offer thanks for all the times we shared in the mornings alone as I fed him. When I'm alone with Oreo I call him "The Big Dog" . . . Yesterday, "The Big Dog" politely declined his meal and has not eaten since. He knows it's time to say goodbye.

With his head still held high, I saw the responsibility for all of us loosen. I will never forget how honorably he quixotically strived to carry the torch for our family. I will bear it into the future remembering his noble and idealistic manner.

My wife and my stepchildren are in the basement curled next to Oreo tonight, the final night of his time living with us.

Tomorrow we will seek mercy for our beloved friend.

Tomorrow night, I will grieve the loss of my brave and loyal buddy. I will miss him so much.

And someday, somewhere I will hope to see him again.

Old School vs. New School

I started and finished my career in the employ of others.

The bulk of my working life was spent on an exploration into free enterprise and capitalism via self-employment. I drove the boat; sometimes the water was smooth, other times the water was pretty choppy. On more than one occasion the boat even capsized but I always got the rudder back in the water and the boat back on course. The corporate world had some subtle changes on either side. Coincidentally, I began and ended my time in the workforce with five-year corporate bookends. Had I not returned for one last five-year dance, I would have missed a very interesting change to the old standard corporate "waltz" I used to know.

The thoughts I express in the following lines are mine and while my meanderings about the subject are sincere, I offer them as nothing more than simple observations.

Let me begin my saying that from my position today, I am and always will be grateful for any and every opportunity that every employer gave me.

I hold the majority of the people I encountered in the highest personal regard.

Okay, okay, okay … I wouldn't give a few of them the time of day, but only for the one characteristic each of the aforementioned few had in common … that they loved money and they used people.

I don't like that.

I never will.

No compromise.

I was a post WWII baby, born in the early 1950s ... an early "Baby Boomer."

The result of my arrival on the scene as a child born in the 1950s was life in America's "traditional" plan. If capable, go to college. Get a job. Work there for forty years. Take your two-week vacation at a Howard Johnson's motel somewhere in Florida during the hottest time of the summer, preferably somewhere in the vicinity of an approaching storm. Retire with a pension from the only place you ever worked. Live out your days. Die ... and do your best to "look like yourself" while doing it.

Yep, that was still the way it was done when I started in the workplace ... just thirty-five or forty years ago.

When I started my career, the traditional career model was just beginning to change. It was the beginning of the end of that business model. I went to college and got a job. Then I, along with my classmates, ushered in the official end of the previous era.

Nixon was still in office.

Enough said.

I spent five years working hard before I left the corporate scene the first time to take a shot at going into business for myself. Something was churning inside me that I couldn't identify ... so, being unable to determine what my inner voice was trying to urge me to do, I ended up staying with my first employer a couple years longer that I should have.

For a while, it was a lot of fun and we all prospered, then suddenly ... it was just painfully boring ... initially, from the retirement of several beloved associates who were mentors in leadership, as well as peers. I was sad from the change. These wonderful souls remain legends for the positive (and, I admit it ... not so positive) influences each of them provided in a personal and genuine effort to help a kid get started. They gave me all they had. The spark that started the passion for me to work, play, learn, and earn in this company had been extinguished. The new leadership didn't have the same drive or capacity to motivate and certainly didn't know how to have fun while doing so. Business here became mundane … that is, more of the same ol', same ol' … again, without the ones who had made it all fun while we all prospered.

I found my restlessness confusing.

I just knew I didn't want to do what I was doing anymore.

Time to leave.

Right out of the gate in my entrepreneurial debut, I failed … just bombed.

The puzzle was too big and I never could get past the edges of it. I tried to run before I could walk.

I was too innocent, too inexperienced, and too … a lot of other things.

And, while frustrating at the time … I didn't quit.

From a long-term perspective it was the best thing that could have happened to me. I received a completely different kind of education.

Failure was very humbling.

Yet … I felt very liberated, as though I had taken a step that many before me had to take as well … as though it was required for the refining process.

I never looked back.

So as an old friend once said when he encountered something similar, "I just looked around in the trunk of my car until I found another idea to try"!

I learned from my mistakes.

My initial failure was a strong asset.

I never gave up. My entrepreneurial spirit was rewarded. For the next twenty-odd years I was rewarded with the contentment of being independent.

However, an old friend in my industry kept professionally seeking to engage me as a part of his multinational conglomerate in a geographically appealing leadership role. I would be able to move back home. After months of consideration, a mutually beneficial solution was reached and I accepted my friend's offer. I was ready to stick my toe back into the water of the corporate side of life.

I would dedicate myself and give the job every ounce of my effort just to see if I could still do the corporate routine again in the 21st century marketplace. I believed it would take that (amount of effort) to satisfy myself and provide my employer with a successful return on their investment (me).

From first glimpse, everything corporate still looked the same from the outside as it did thirty-five years ago.

Dark suits, power ties, button-down collars, wing tips, tassel loafers, and all of that nonsense we're all still stuck with and nobody seems to understand why ... I hadn't had a suit and tie on in twenty-five years except to go to church, funerals, or weddings.

One evident and very visible change is that now there are more competent females in leadership roles ... I saluted, applauded, respected, and fully embraced that change.

In business, regardless of a company's product or the era in which it is sold, a solid plan that is concisely organized will always be mandated to have any chance of success. That organized plan exists so that it may be executed in such a way that when careful controls are surrounding the plan's overall concept, the results yield maximum profits.

Let me elaborate. In all of my business experience, self-employed or not, there are four absolute, basic "carved in stone" steps involved in a solid business plan that will yield maximum profits. There is the "Old School" way I experienced thirty-five years ago, and then there is the "New School" way that I experienced the last five years of my career.

I learned these four steps from a wise old owl I met in a barn a long time ago.

The four-steps are:

1. Plan
2. Organize

3. Execute

4. Control

The difference, to me, between Old School and New School is the percentage of effort focused on the last two steps listed above, 3. Execute and 4. Control.

However, it's the biggest change I noticed between the two "schools."

Basically, the Old School corporate world wanted to execute its plan to gain maximum revenue. Control was necessary in order to generate maximum profits from the execution of the plan … I understood.

Reciprocally, by every appearance to me, the New School corporate world seems to want, require, and demand control so as to "maximize the pursuit" of revenue and profits. Execution was necessary only as it met the criteria set forth by the control established for the organized business plan … frankly, I didn't understand.

My comments in the previous few paragraphs boil down to this:

Old School says you execute eighty percent of the time and make sure everything sold is in alignment with the initial organized plan to maximize profits by implementing control twenty percent of the time.

New School says you execute twenty percent of the time and make sure everything sold is in alignment with the initial organized plan to maximize profits by implementing control eighty percent of the time.

Metaphorically speaking, what appears to have happened in the past few decades can best be summed up in the following story:

Old School and New School are each on a horse riding to their next appointment side-by-side on the old sales trail. Suddenly, without any explanation, in a simultaneous phenomenon both of their horses fall dead underneath them.

Old School immediately grabs all of his gear and begins walking to the next town. In the town, Old School heads directly to the livery stable and buys another horse and is on his way to his next sales appointment.

Meanwhile, back on the trail, New School stops and wonders why the horse died. It should have lived longer according to specifications. New School then decides that it would be best to avoid such an incident in the future and ascertains there is but one way to do so. New School crawls up the dead horse's fanny to see what killed it. After determining the answer, New School gathers his gear and walks into the next town. Upon entering the next town, New School attempts to engage various townspeople to determine if any of them have had the same issues with any of their horses. New School is repeatedly shunned. New School diligently presses on with his effort to gain information from the marketplace about his dead horse. New School is too preoccupied with his goal of getting their data collected to remember that he has just crawled out of a horse's fanny and doesn't smell very good. As New School relents, he sees the livery stable and goes in search of the owner. New School begins the discussion with the owner, asking him if he's had any problems with horses such as he had back on the trail. The livery stable owner tells New School that he smells like a horse's fanny and he needs to go to the local hotel and take a bath and come back to talk to him tomorrow about any problems he's having. New School apologizes, goes to the hotel, takes a bath, spends the night, gets up, and decides that he would take an hour or two to attempt to gather data again from the townspeople to see if any of them had a similar issue with a horse dying. New School gets back to the livery stable at lunchtime and the owner isn't there, so he proceeds to investigate further with the hired hand until the owner returns. Upon the return of the owner, New School launches back into his investigation that began the previous afternoon when he still smelled like the dead horse's fanny. After a thorough probe and analysis of the livery stable owner, they both come to the conclusion that neither of them had ever seen a horse that indeed had a condition such as the one New School lost back on the trail. The livery stable owner asks New School if he would like to buy another horse. After great debate on exactly which horse to buy, because he didn't want the same thing happening that happened to his horse before, New School relents and buys another horse. However, before New School can be on his way to his next appointment on the old sales trail he stops to send a telegram to his office to arrange an emergency meeting with the management team on Sunday to discuss his prior horse's death and how to handle such issues should they ever arise in the future. Upon the completion of his telegram, he realizes that it is too late to get back on the old sales trail and decides to spend one more night in the local hotel. Bright and early the next day, New School, armed with a load of information in case another horse ever dies on the old sales trail, leaves for his next sales appointment … a full two days later than Old School.

I'll give anybody the benefit of the doubt and explain that I might be missing some elaborate concept somewhere that legitimately scrutinizes my feeble effort to communicate what I have observed and experienced over the last few decades. Again, these are simply my casual yet careful personal observations.

At the end of the day … perhaps …

New School's method might provide the highest long-term company stock share value. Beats me. Personally, I think after a good plan is in place, too damn much thinking, talking, and meeting … and not enough getting up off of your ass and doing … does not increase the law of averages for creating revenue.

Old School's simple method of "bodies in motion stay in motion" fits me much better and I think following a solid plan will create more revenue as a result.

I don't need to sleep on it …

I'm more of an Old School kind of guy.

Collard Greens, Sausage, and Septic Tanks

Choosing to be thankful and happy regardless of my circumstances have been two vitally important decisions in my life.

Sometimes, as I get lost in my thoughts, I like to think about different people who have influenced me. My parents, my wife, neighbors, pastors, teachers, friends, coaches, business associates, peers, and sometimes people I have never personally met who have caused me to want to stop, think, and make myself better. Two of those come to mind ... *The Atlanta Journal-Constitution*'s retired sportswriter Furman Bisher and *The Miami Herald*'s Dave Barry. I have never met either one of these legendary newspapermen. However, both of them, through their words, have given me cause to count them as influential. Every fourth Thursday of November during my life, Furman (who is in his 90s) has always written a column explaining exactly what he is thankful for every Thanksgiving Day. Reading Furman's Thanksgiving column is as big a tradition in my house as eating turkey. Dave (who probably feels like he's in his 90s) never fails to find the humor in anything. Never. I like that.

I am so thankful to have had a career that allowed me to meet so many wonderful people. I have always loved what I did for a living. Regardless of any title on a business card, it has always boiled down to this ... I am a salesman. Spending time with customers regardless of the circumstances has been financially rewarding, interesting, and fun. I'm thankful for each and every one of them. I can't think of one that doesn't bring a smile to my heart. Rarely a day goes by that I don't laugh out loud about experiences with old customers or former associates. They are like an extended family. I love them.

One of the many joys of working with small business owners is the level of personal relationships that form over the years. Seems like all I ever did was ride around, see people, chew the fat, write down some numbers on a piece of paper, and then have them sign it. Two weeks later there was money in my paycheck. I know there was more to it than that, but looking back, that's really what it amounted to. The clients got products or services they needed for their businesses to help them prosper; I got commissions for helping them fill their needs.

Not just the customers have had a profound influence on me. Early in my career, an old guy nicknamed "Hawkins" who had a nose shaped like a ski slope once told me a secret, "You've just got to care the most to sell the most . . . you really have to give a damn, son. Nothing less will do. Anything less is unacceptable and won't be tolerated." He only told me once. He thought that once was enough. Have you ever had a boss that you couldn't stand but you knew was right? Hawkins was cranky ... hell, Hawkins was borderline impossible ... but he was right. Hawkins led by example. He would never ask you to do anything that he wasn't willing to do first. There wasn't a lazy bone in his body. There are good managers and there are good leaders and believe me, there is a difference. Hawkins was a leader. He didn't have the best bedside manner, but he had your best interest in mind. I am a better and happier man because of the things he taught me.

Remember my old happiness mentor, Luther? Well, Hawkins was a classmate of Luther's in college and Luther always told me, "If you can tolerate the cranky old soul, he will help you. Just use him; that's what he's here for." Luther was right, too. Oh yeah ... by the way, Luther gave Hawkins his nickname. And for what it's worth, Luther had plenty of lazy bones ... he used Hawkins every chance he got! Did I mention that Luther was one smart old goat?

It took a decade or so for me to realize the truth and wisdom in Hawkins' words. By the time I realized their value, Hawkins and Luther were no longer involved in my daily professional activities. Luther died in 1990. I believe the last time I saw Hawkins was at Luther's funeral. Spiritually, they have remained right by my side, whispering tidbits of truth and wisdom from my stored memories of them every day.

Over the past thirty-five years, wonderful memories linger. I have had priceless experiences with customers. Sure, I helped clients make money. But since when was that the answer to everything ... especially to Luther and our old boss, stubborn, bull-headed, pain in the ass, "it's my way or the highway" Hawkins. They both taught me well. Do things right. Accept nothing less than your best from yourself. Things get personal with small business people. You provide services and products to help them; they open their hearts to you.

Customers have invited me to participate in their church, civic, and family lives.

I have been there when countless numbers of children and grandchildren were born.

I have been to music recitals.

I have been to dance recitals.

I have been to beauty contests.

I have been to their children's basketball games, wrestling matches, baseball games, gymnastic matches, track meets, and football games.

I've even been to out-of-town high school football games over 200 miles away when I didn't get home until four o'clock in the morning.

I've been to a golf tournament where I sat under a tent while it rained for four hours and never saw one of the kids from the customer's son's school because the bus they were coming on broke down on the way to the event and had to be towed home.

They forfeited. I never even saw a putt.

I have been to kindergarten, elementary, middle, and high school graduations.

I have attended college graduations.

I have attended post-graduate commencement ceremonies.

I have been to many dozens of weddings.

I have consoled the pains of dozens of divorces.

They have consoled me as well.

I have been hunting with customers.

I have been fishing with customers.

I have played countless rounds of golf with customers.

I have played tennis with customers.

I have bungee jumped with customers.

I have parasailed with customers.

I have snorkeled in the open ocean with customers.

I have attended about a hundred rounds of golf at "The Masters" tournament in Augusta. Tickets weren't always as hard to get as they are today.

I have watched World Series games with customers.

I have watched Super Bowls with customers.

I have been to countless ballgames at Georgia, Georgia Tech, Alabama, Virginia, Notre Dame, Auburn, Virginia Tech, Tennessee, Florida, Florida State, Clemson, Miami, LSU, South Carolina, Arkansas, North Carolina, Duke, Kentucky, Ole Miss, Vanderbilt, and Mississippi State. These were the customers' favorite teams.

Atlanta Braves games with customers, hundreds!

Atlanta Falcons game with customers, dozens!

I have gone on family vacations with customers. Only once … ouch!

I have been to and spoken at Lions, Rotary, and Kiwanis Clubs, and even a Daughters of the American Revolution meeting, just to mention a few.

I have been to places that I am ashamed to say I've been with customers.

I've closed bars with customers.

I've been to Las Vegas with customers.

I've been to New Orleans with customers.

God help me, I've driven a customer a couple hundred miles to Panama City Beach, Florida just to eat oysters one afternoon.

I have attended a service of every denomination of the Protestant church with customers.

Some customers took me to church services that were in different languages.

I have had customers come with me to my church.

I have been to Catholic churches with customers.

I have attended Temple with Jewish customers.

I once attended a Hindu Temple with a client. Afterwards, we ate the spiciest food on the planet and I consumed an entire bottle of Mylanta antacid before the next morning. They said yogurt would have been a better solution ... so, I ate some yogurt for breakfast.

I've carried the caskets of customers to their final resting place and buried a part of my heart with them.

These kinds of things just went with the job of caring about the people you were working alongside to try to help them while scratching out a living for yourself. It all just went with caring.

"You really have to give a damn, son." Thanks, Hawkins ... believe it or not, I heard every word you said. Call it "Old School." Call it corny if you choose ... it made for a wonderful past thirty-five years in the marketplace.

My customers showed me how much they cared when I became seriously ill. I received much more than I ever dreamed possible during my ordeal with brain cancer. I heard from countless customers extending their love and concern. I had no idea how much all of us meant to one another. I can summarize their concern about my health with one example.

An old cabinet-maker, "Herk" Siebert, had a cabinet shop on Wilmington Island near Savannah. When he heard of my illness with brain cancer, his wife, Margaret, told me he went to his shop alone one night and with his tools he intricately carved a gift for me. He didn't come back for hours. Margaret said that when he returned she could tell that he'd been crying. Herk had done a freehand carving of two kneeling angels leaning towards one another. The outside of their wings formed the shape of a heart. With the words "Peace Dave" carved at their feet, the angels still greet me every morning of my life reminding me of how blessed I have been to have had such wonderful friends during my career. Herk's carving hangs in my sunroom window today as one of my most cherished possessions.

But, by far the greatest privilege of getting personally close to clients is when they invite you into their homes.

It is always for the same reason. FOOD. They have a particular special dish that they have and they want to feed you. Don't we always want to feed the ones we love?

What I wouldn't give for just one more plate of fried shrimp and hush puppies from Edwina and Junior Redd's kitchen, cooked using lard in her black cast iron skillet.

One of my favorite memories involved a septic tank business. I was riding with one of our company's reps that day and our last call involved seeing the folks who owned the septic tank establishment to sell them some advertising. The sale was somewhat of a foregone conclusion, as they had been customers for years. So while the rep was writing the business for their advertising program, I reverted to my Old School habit of just shooting the breeze with them. After the client had shown me the new hunting rifle his wife had recently bought him, the subject of food was inevitably brought up.

It was as simple as him asking me, "Do you like pork sausage?"

Well, Lord yes, I like pork sausage! He proceeded to explain that the family had just had a hog killed and wanted both the rep and me to take a couple pounds of fresh sausage home with us.

Normally, that would have been a typical end of the story, but his wife heard what was going on (we were sitting at their dining room table) and peeked around the corner from the kitchen and asked, "How are you going to cook your sausage?" My response was that I would make it into patties and fry it to eat with eggs this Saturday morning.

And she responded, "Do y'all like collards?"

You guessed it, out of the kitchen she came with a bowl full of the best collards mixed with fresh ground pork sausage you could imagine. My rep and I made ourselves right at home and enjoyed the meal, which was one of the most amazing combinations of flavor I have ever eaten. Onions sautéed in the drippings of bacon, homemade chicken stock as a base, the fresh collards added and cooked down with some sugar in a cast iron pot before adding in the fresh and lightly-spiced cooked ground sausage.

Incredible food. Just incredible!

When we finished, the septic tank folks sent us home with leftovers for our meals the next day, with our sausage, with their recipe for collard greens and sausage, and with another year's advertising program. And most importantly, with the kind assurance that the "Old School" way of doing business based on trust, relationships, and helping each other profit still works today!

I wish you could smell the collard greens and sausage cooking, Hawkins. I wish you could share a bowl with me, I really do. If it weren't for you and Luther, I would've never known about 'em. Every chance I've been given to lead in my career, you and your wisdom from my experiences along with you as a young man (I can still feel your passionate reprimands) finds a way to shine through into my words and actions. You'll never know how much you taught me just letting me look over your shoulder. You were the best. I thought you might be a long time ago … I know you are today.

Uncle Charlie's Magical Mystery Tour

Daddy's baby sister, Mary, married Uncle Charlie after a six-week whirlwind courtship in the late 1940s. They were married a couple of years before Mama and Daddy met in the winter of 1949. They had four daughters—Sharon, Cindy, Cathy, and Mary Lillian.

Their family lived together in New Haven, Connecticut, my Daddy's hometown.

Mama, Daddy, my little brother, Phil, and I took two trips to Connecticut to see Aunt Mary, Uncle Charlie, and the girls in the 1960s. These two trips were the only family vacations that I ever remember all four of us taking together. They were special times for us. The last trip was in the summer of 1969, before my senior year in high school.

The trip in the summer of 1969 was my last memory of seeing Uncle Charlie, Aunt Mary, and their girls together.

Uncle Charlie and Aunt Mary made frequent efforts to be around whenever they passed through Georgia and occasionally we would see one of their girls.

Uncle Charlie was the most generous relative I had. Even though he lived almost a thousand miles away, he spent time with me. The time he spent alone with me was the most important thing he ever gave me. He came to visit me several times when I was in college. We played countless rounds of golf together and he gave me most of the golf clubs I ever used. He came to stay with us after I was married and became the personal secret advisor to both of my sons, coaching them regarding their interest in the opposite sex. He was the one that bought them their first copy of "Playboy" magazine. My boys really loved their great Uncle Charlie. His presence was the most valuable gift he ever offered. Uncle Charlie loved me. He didn't have to tell me ... actions speak louder than words.

I got the call from Mama as I was riding back from a business meeting with an associate late on a Friday afternoon in July 2008. Uncle Charlie had died. He had been sick with a cruel disease for the last couple of years. His suffering was over. His funeral would take place the following Wednesday.

Aunt Mary fell ill the year before and died after a brief illness. Because of my health issues I wasn't able to make the trip to her funeral. Phil had taken my parents. They flew to Aunt Mary's memorial service.

Mama was concerned about her and Daddy's ability to travel by air to Uncle Charlie's funeral. They were old and didn't need or want to deal with the hassle of airports and arthritis. They are both well over eighty and weren't confident of their ability to drive that far either.

I called my brother. He had a vacation planned for his family around business meetings that he couldn't cancel on such short notice. I told him not to think about it again; I would figure out the best way to get them there.

My business associate who was riding with me at the time of the call heard all of the conversations. He and I are the same age; coincidentally, he is from Connecticut, too. He asked what had happened and expressed his concern for the loss of my uncle.

Then he simply said, "Why don't you just take the week off, drive up the back way through the Shenandoah Valley on I-81, you know the way ... it's such a beautiful ride, show your parents all around New England and enjoy the time you have with them. When will you ever have a chance to do something like this with your Mom and Dad again? Your Uncle Charlie wouldn't have it any other way."

He was right ... my quiet, witty, loving, funny, and generous Uncle Charlie wouldn't have had it any other way.

I called Mama and told her to have their suitcases packed and ready to go. I would pick them up on Saturday morning. They were pleased and excited to be going on a trip together with me.

I have traveled extensively throughout New England and knew the area well. Our plan was to see every state in the region and end up in New Haven for Charlie's memorial service.

I drove, Daddy rode "shotgun" in the front seat with me, and Mama had the entire back seat to herself. On our way through the Shenandoah Valley Saturday afternoon we encountered a heavy thunderstorm. The sun emerged and shone brightly through the rain and suddenly a brilliant rainbow appeared. We were driving along "in" the end of the rainbow.

I will never forget Daddy turning to me and asking, "Have you ever seen anything like this?" ... I hadn't. What a sight it was to watch my eighty-three-year-old Daddy reaching towards the windshield, marveling that his arm was bathed in the rainbow's colors. It was magical.

This was going to be a special trip.

Somebody somewhere was watching over our journey.

We drove to southern Pennsylvania the first night.

Sunday morning, we drove through the Amish countryside in Pennsylvania and saw a horse and buggy riding along in traffic. Daddy was like a kid. "Look, Helen!"

We crossed the Hudson River north of New York City around midday and continued up the beautiful Taconic Parkway until we crossed into Massachusetts. The first quintessential New England village we entered was Great Barrington, Massachusetts. Everywhere you looked was like a postcard sent from the local chamber of commerce beckoning you to come and visit. We also went through Stockbridge, Massachusetts, Norman Rockwell's hometown.

Mom and Dad were mesmerized by the beauty of the towns in the Berkshire Mountains of western Massachusetts.

Okay, I have always been a "Son of the South," a straight-from-the-dirt-road Georgia boy, but this is some seriously pretty country.

I didn't know until three years ago, on the way to Uncle Charlie's funeral, how close I came to being raised in New England instead of my beloved Georgia.

Mama and Daddy were married over sixty years ago on August 25, 1950.

They were married in a small country church in Forsyth County, Georgia, on a hot August night. They have spent the last sixty years together living in five different houses, none more than a few miles apart from the other in and around the Atlanta area. My childhood was spent in the first three of these homes.

Daddy said that when he came to Georgia to meet Mama's family for the first time, he knew he would never be able to go home to Connecticut to live again.

He couldn't possibly ever ask her to leave her family.

But, that Sunday in Stockbridge, my Mama said to Daddy while gazing in wonder at the quaint beauty surrounding her, "Lee, if you'd brought me up here in 1950, showed me all of these places, and asked me to move up North with you ... I would have."

Daddy responded, "Lord have mercy, Helen, I've never seen any of this before either ... if I had known all of this was up here I might have never left! We never did anything but ride the train from New Haven to New York and back."

It's only eighty miles from New Haven to Stockbridge. If Daddy had brought Mama just eighty miles farther sixty years ago ... well, I wouldn't have my Southern drawl, I never would've been an Atlanta Braves fan, and I probably would've gone to college at Amherst or Williams instead of Furman.

Whew, that was close. I have no idea how to shovel snow!

I loved my Aunt Mary, Uncle Charlie, and their lovely girls and I really do like traveling in New England, but I stand by my convictions ... I'm a

"Son of the South." Thank God for Mama having such a close and loving family back in North Georgia.

We traveled throughout New England as planned.

For the first time in their lives, Mama and Daddy saw the breathtaking Connecticut River Valley which forms the border between Vermont and New Hampshire; Ethan Allen and his "Green Mountain Boys'" legendary refuge in Vermont; the picturesque campus of Dartmouth College in Hanover; the White Mountains' majestic Mount Washington in Bretton Woods, New Hampshire; the rustic cabins that surround Lake Sebago; and the presidential rocky seaside village of Kennebunkport, Maine.

It was in Kennebunkport that Mama grew quiet and said that she felt a little guilty about having so much fun on a trip that was initiated as the result of Charlie's death. We remained a little quieter than before as we drove to New Haven. A reverent spirit had joined us on our last leg of our journey to bid Uncle Charlie farewell.

At his memorial service, Charlie's girls had a celebration of their Dad's life. He would have been so proud of them. He always was.

It was a beautiful day to be with our family.

On the ride back to Atlanta, Daddy began to think out loud and reviewed our week together ... as we all rode and remembered, Mama spoke up and said, "Charlie would've enjoyed knowing that we had so much fun together..."

Yep, Uncle Charlie ... you outdid yourself this time.

You waited to give me the best gift you ever gave me until after you were gone. I know you're smiling somewhere.

Yep ... my quiet, witty, loving, funny, and generous Uncle Charlie wouldn't have had it any other way.

"Thanks for Giving a Damn"

"When von Hugel, the great philosopher, mystic and saint, lay dying, he tried to speak but he was so weak that the family members could not hear what he was trying to say. One of them leaned close to his lips and heard him whisper, "Caring is everything. Nothing matters but caring."

~ Dr. Garnett Wilder

I saw the above quote on a church bulletin of a service I attended at First Methodist, Athens, Georgia, in 1996. Dr. Wilder was a hero of mine. He was a totally no-nonsense guy. He was at my side the entire time I battled brain cancer. He was my pastor. He was a tough old buzzard. I loved his style. He told me in no uncertain terms that he worshiped a God who kept his promises, but that I had to find the promises and claim them as my own.

I have kept the copy of that order of service in my Bible for fifteen years. I have thought of Garnett's quote often. I've been waiting for the right time to use it. I woke up in the middle of the night last night and knew I'd found the time and place that was right to share his quote.

Garnett would approve.

Garnett died nobly while in a pulpit caring many years ago. His last words as he looked over the congregation were an emphatic declaration. Before he sat down, slumped forward, and died ... Garnett boldly implored the congregation to "Trust God!"

Garnett cared.

I retired from the advertising and publishing industry three years ago.

They gave me a nice going away dinner at a local restaurant.

Thankfully, I think the days of giving somebody a gold watch when they retire are long gone. The last thing I need now is a watch. I don't care what time it is. And if I did care what time it was, the phone in my pocket has a clock that keeps time better than any watch I've ever owned.

They invited people from all around the state to my retirement dinner and explained that any attendees would be responsible for the purchase of their own dinner if they chose to come. They made sure that everyone who came really cared about me. Wow, the corporate gang kept the potential moochers looking for a free steak from coming to the party.

The leadership in the company had this gig figured out! Smooth move, eh? Naturally, they paid the check for everyone.

People came from all around.

I was touched.

When the meal was finished, there were notes, cards, books, golf balls, fishing lures, and (of course) a stupid plaque to wade through. It was a special and memorable night. There were many jokes, lots of laughter, and some tears also.

It's official. All I have now is time on my hands. I'm really glad they didn't give me a gold watch. The memories of our fellowship together are far sweeter.

The next morning I was reading the cards and notes again and a particular one touched me the most.

It was a "Thank You" card, blank on the inside except for his written words. I had directly supervised or counseled this fine man throughout my tenure at the company.

Upon opening the card, there was one written line, "Thanks for giving a damn ... Brian."

Compiling the stories of *Dirt Roads and Daydreams* has occupied a corner of my mind for a long time. I have wondered for years why I felt so compelled to write this book with its colloquial title and yet not done it. First, the time—it's taken two years; second, I've never had the support in place that I have now to be able to recall and write; and finally, I haven't stopped finding people to be thankful for. I never will.

All of the folks ... heck, all of the animals in the book are real. No names are changed.

The stories I've shared with you from the time I was a toddler until today have been vitally important in the survival and healing process for any illnesses or adversities I have faced in my life. My faith, my family, my friends, having fun, and being a useful, productive person have genuinely been the most amazing medicine of all.

There are so very many people who have gone on from this life that I can never repay; some that I simply can't recall ... all of whom took their time to "give a damn" about me, a never-ending daydreamer who really came from those dirt roads.

I wanted to remember them all, past or present, as best I could with personal stories and experiences we shared together along the dusty paths that molded me into the person I have become.

Each of them has made a difference by their caring in their own particular way. All cared so much.

Since I left my beloved dirt roads and their daydreams I have been surrounded by a circle of devoted people who have cared about me. Their love and care drives within me a deep passion to care also. I offer my humble thanks for being led to care.

From the bottom of my heart ...

"Thanks for giving a damn."